AnimalWays

Frogs

AnimalWays

Frogs

Dan Greenberg

BENCHMARK BOOKS

MARSHALL CAVENDISH
NEW YORK

With thanks to Paul Sieswerda of the New York Aquarium
for his expert reading of this manuscript.

Benchmark Books
Marshall Cavendish Corporation
99 White Plains Road
Tarrytown, NY 10591-9001

Library of Congress Cataloging-in-Publication Data
Greenberg, Daniel A.
Frogs / by Dan Greenberg.
       p. cm.—(Animal ways)
Summary: Describes the physical characteristics, behavior, habitat, and various species
of frogs.
ISBN 0-7614-1138-0
1. Frogs—Juvenile literature. [1. Frogs.] I. Title. II. Animal ways (Tarrytown, N.Y.)
QL668.E2 G72   2001   597.8'9—dc21   99-058371

Photo research by Candlepants, Inc.

Cover photo: The National Audubon Society Collection / Photo Researchers, Inc.: Jacana

The photographs in this book are used by permission and through the courtesy of: *The
National Audubon Society Collection/Photo Researchers, Inc.*: Tom McHugh, 2, 40, 75, 87;
Cosmos Blank, 9; Tim Davis, 10, 67; Frans Lanting, 16; Volker Steger/Science Photo
Library, 21; Gary Retherford, 23; Michael Lustbader, 25, 81; Dr. Paul A. Zahl, 32 (top left),
95 (bottom), back cover; C. K. Lorenz, 32 (bottom), 55, 59, 91; Gregory G. Dimijian, 33
(middle), 42, 69, 101; Stephen Dalton, 35, 45; David T. Roberts, 39, 77; Roger Wilmhurst,
47; Jim Goodwin, 49; Merlin Tuttle, 52; Rod Planck, 53; J. T. Collins, 56; Karl H. Switak, 58;
Kenneth H. Thomas, 60, 85; Jeffrey Lepore, 62, 65; Michael McCoy, 78; Maslowski, 83;
Wayne Lawler, 89; Richard R. Hansen, 90; E. R. Degginger, 93; Suzanne L. Collins, 95
(top); S. & J. Collins, 96. *A. B. Sheldon*: 32 (top right), 33 (top left & right), 33 (bottom).
Dan Suzio: 70 (71, 70 (bottom left & right), 71 (top). 71 (middle left & right), 71 (bottom).

Printed in Italy

6 5 4 3 2 1

Contents

Animal Kingdom

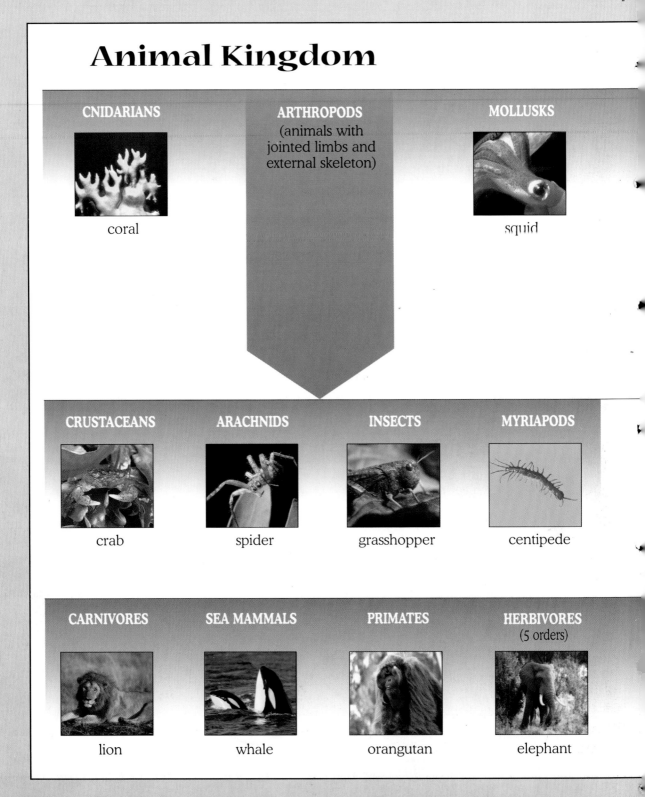

CNIDARIANS

coral

ARTHROPODS
(animals with jointed limbs and external skeleton)

MOLLUSKS

squid

CRUSTACEANS

crab

ARACHNIDS

spider

INSECTS

grasshopper

MYRIAPODS

centipede

CARNIVORES

lion

SEA MAMMALS

whale

PRIMATES

orangutan

HERBIVORES
(5 orders)

elephant

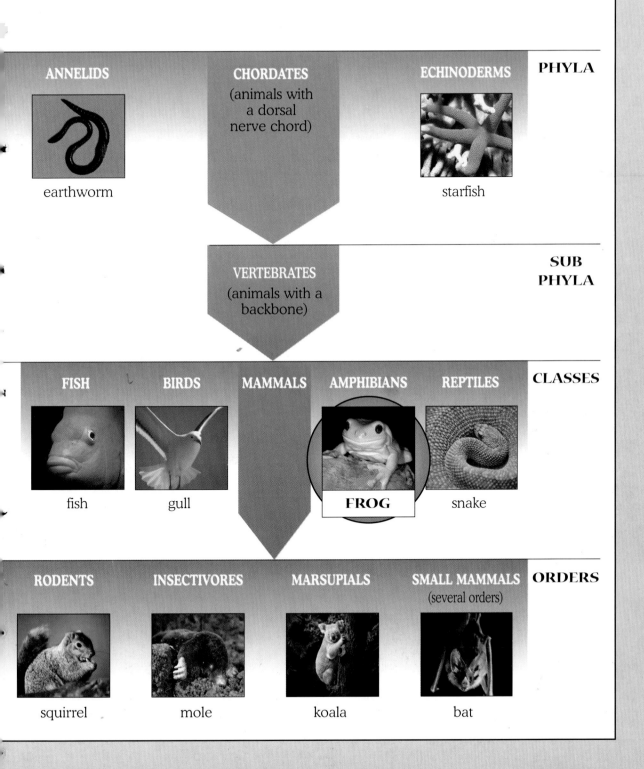

PHYLA

ANNELIDS

earthworm

CHORDATES
(animals with
a dorsal
nerve chord)

ECHINODERMS

starfish

SUB PHYLA

VERTEBRATES
(animals with a
backbone)

CLASSES

FISH

fish

BIRDS

gull

MAMMALS

AMPHIBIANS

FROG

REPTILES

snake

ORDERS

RODENTS

squirrel

INSECTIVORES

mole

MARSUPIALS

koala

SMALL MAMMALS
(several orders)

bat

1 The World of Frogs

> "HO HO!" SAID THE TOAD, "WHAT A CLEVER TOAD
> I AM. THERE IS SURELY NO ANIMAL EQUAL TO ME
> FOR CLEVERNESS IN THE WHOLE WORLD!"
>
> from *The Wind in the Willows*, Kenneth Grahame

It's a quiet day at the pond. The sun shines and birds chirp. Insects buzz overhead. All the while, the frog sits on a lily pad, waiting.

Before long, a bee comes into range. The frog waits, then suddenly attacks. Its long tongue, coated with sticky mucus, flips out, striking its victim in midair. Then the tongue curls back, bringing the insect into the frog's gaping mouth.

The action unfolds at a speed faster than the human eye can follow. The actual sequence of events can be captured only

A FROG STRIKES FROM A LILY PAD.

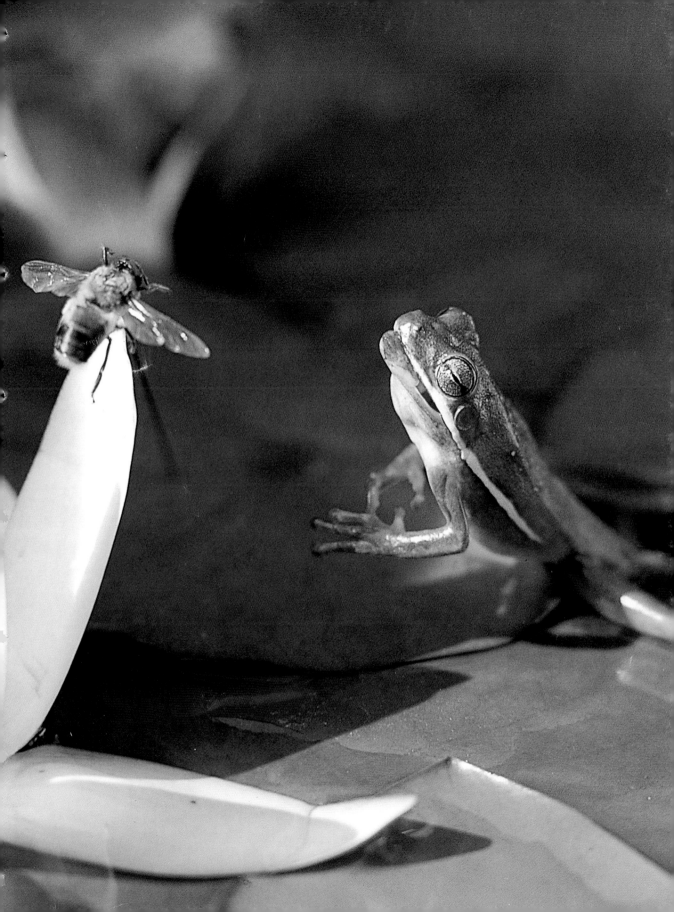

THE RED-EYED TREE FROG IS ONE OF MANY FROGS TO TAKE UP RESIDENCE IN THE
TREES. MANY TREE FROGS SPEND THEIR ENTIRE ADULT LIVES WITHOUT GOING
UNDERWATER.

by using high-speed photography. Nevertheless, a single frog is likely to reenact this hyper-speed drama dozens of times in a typical day.

IF YOU SPEND TIME AT A LOCAL POND, YOU ARE LIKELY TO VIEW A SCENE much like the one described above. Frogs make up a vital part of most freshwater habitats. They are found on every continent on Earth, from Alaska to the Andes Mountains, from Sweden to the Himalayas.

Typically living in wet habitats, frogs inhabit ponds, lakes, rivers, marshes, and streams. Frogs also have been able to adapt to less moist environments such as forests, grasslands, and in some cases, even deserts.

How did frogs come to be so successful? Variety is one key. Frogs come in an astonishing number of sizes, shapes, and colors. Some frogs are poisonous. Other frogs can fly through the air. (Actually, they glide.) Still other frogs are the Michael Jordans of the animal world, leaping twenty or more times their body length in a single bound.

The other key to the great success of frogs in colonizing so many parts of the world is their ability to find warm, moist spots in otherwise cool or dry locations. For example, though many frog species make the forest their home, they are rarely seen. Instead, frogs stay hidden where it is wet and warm, crouching in a mass of damp leaves or perching high in the trees under branches where water droplets condense. In other habitats frogs occupy similar niches. No matter what their home environment, frogs have the unfailing ability to find the warmth and wetness they need to survive.

In all, scientists have identified at least 3,500 different kinds of frogs. Each year, new species are discovered, so the count may someday reach 4,000. This array of species includes everything from the tiny .39-inch (1-cm) Cuban frog to the gigantic African goliath frog, which measures over 15 inches (40 cm) in length—roughly the size of a large pepperoni pizza!

Frog Habitats

Most frogs are restricted to habitats that are both warm and wet. Frogs need warmth because, like all amphibians, they are ectotherms, or cold-blooded animals. Ectotherms cannot regulate their temperature using their own body heat. To get the energy they need to be active, ectotherms need to obtain warmth from outside. Endotherms such as mammals, on the other hand, generate enough body heat from burning food to stay active and so maintain a constant body temperature. Because they are ectotherms, amphibians tend to inhabit places with relatively warm climates.

Amphibians breathe through their skin. Oxygen and carbon dioxide can diffuse, or spread, through skin only if it is wet. To stay wet, amphibians must continually get water from the environment. This limits them to habitats that are near or in water.

Amphibians also need water to breed. The first vertebrates, or animals with backbones, to take up life on land, amphibians have strong ties to the watery world of their ancestors. While many amphibians have adapted to a life on land as adults, almost all of them must return to water to lay eggs. The eggs of most frogs hatch into tadpoles, which spend the first stage of their lives as aquatic creatures that have gills instead of lungs. Only after tadpoles become adult frogs and develop lungs are they able to survive on land.

Given their need to stay warm and wet, the diversity of environments in which frogs can be found is remarkable. However, while some frogs have managed to survive in harsh

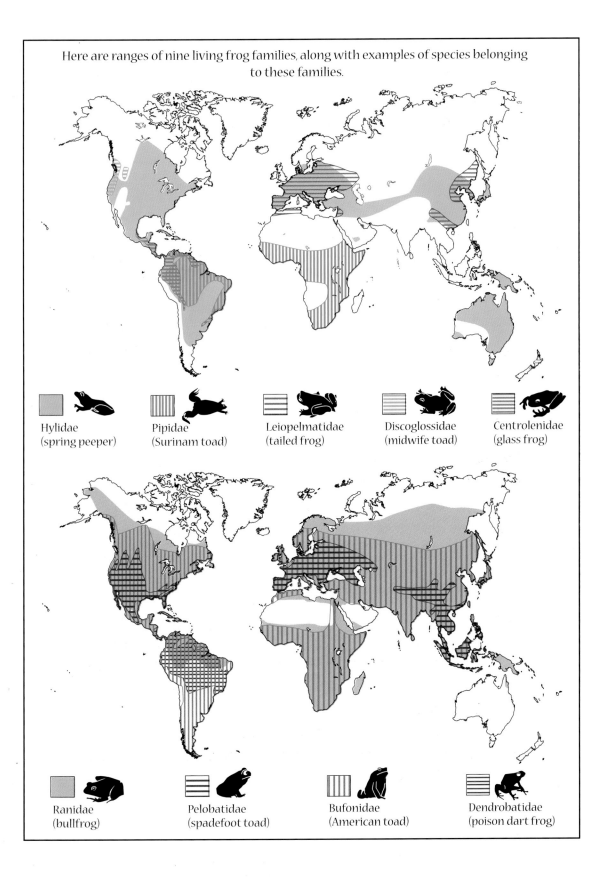

Here are ranges of nine living frog families, along with examples of species belonging to these families.

Hylidae
(spring peeper)

Pipidae
(Surinam toad)

Leiopelmatidae
(tailed frog)

Discoglossidae
(midwife toad)

Centrolenidae
(glass frog)

Ranidae
(bullfrog)

Pelobatidae
(spadefoot toad)

Bufonidae
(American toad)

Dendrobatidae
(poison dart frog)

environments, most frog species live in warm, humid, tropical climates. Great Britain, for example, with its cool climate, has only five different frog species, while only a few acres of the hot, wet rain forest of Ecuador houses over eighty-three.

Frogs as Amphibians

Frogs and toads are amphibians. The word *amphibian* comes from two Greek words, *amphi* (both) and *bios* (life), and refers to something that functions equally well both on land and in water. Thus, an amphibious vehicle can drive on land or move through water. Amphibious soldiers are trained for both land and sea missions. And amphibian life-forms live a dual existence—partly on land and partly in the water.

Amphibians, like other animal groups, have a unique position in the classification system used to organize all living things on Earth. The system divides life-forms into six kingdoms: bacteria, a bacteria-like group, single-celled organisms, fungi, plants, and animals. The animal kingdom is divided into separate groups called phyla. Major phyla include such groups as the arthropods (insects, crabs), mollusks (clams, squid), echinoderms (starfish), and chordates, or animals with nerve cords.

Amphibians belong to a major chordate group called the vertebrates, or animals with backbones. Amphibians are only one of several vertebrate classes. Other well-known vertebrate classes include sharks and rays, bony fish, reptiles, birds, and mammals. Amphibians are thought to be the first tetrapods, or four-limbed animals, to have appeared on Earth.

The amphibians' closest vertebrate relatives are the reptiles. People often confuse amphibians with reptiles. Both are cold-blooded. And superficially, some members of the two groups do look alike. But they differ in key ways.

Most reptiles are fully terrestrial organisms while most amphibians live partly on land and partly in water. Reptiles are able to survive on land for two primary reasons. First, they have dry, scaly, waterproof skin that does not need to be kept wet like amphibian skin. This allows reptiles to escape the need to be near water at all times.

The reptilian egg was the second adaptation, or acquired trait, that allowed reptiles to become land animals. Amphibians lay "naked" eggs that dry up if they are not deposited in water. Reptiles, on the other hand, lay eggs with an amniotic layer that functions like a "pond in a pocket." Amniotic eggs have a watery medium that provides an environment in which the embryo can develop and a hard outer shell that protects the embryo and keeps it from drying out. Amniotic eggs allowed reptiles to breed on land and so become the first fully terrestrial organisms.

What is a Frog?

Frogs are easy to recognize but hard to define. Generally speaking, frogs are tailless amphibians. The tailless amphibians make up one of the three main amphibian groups. The other two amphibian orders include the wormlike caecilians and the newt, salamander, and siren group. Frogs and toads form a group called Anura, which comes from the Greek word for "tailless ones."

One source of confusion in the world of tailless amphibians is the difference between frogs and toads. Simply speaking, toads are frogs. But frogs are not toads. Here's why: all tailless amphibians are lumped under the single heading of frogs, and toads make up one family within this group. In all, there are at least twenty-one frog families. The most well known of these in the temperate United States are the Ranids, or "true" frogs, and the Bufonids, or "true" toads. Worldwide, there are almost seven

THIS GIANT TOAD BELONGS TO THE BUFONIDAE FAMILY—THE "TRUE" TOADS—WHICH
IS ONE OF THE TWENTY-ONE FROG FAMILIES.

AMPHIBIANS

salamanders,
newts, sirens

caecilians

FROGS ·············· clawed frogs

TRUE TOADS

spadefoot toads

ghost frogs

"true" frogs

tree frogs

poison dart frogs

reed frogs

others—21 frog
    families in all

**FROG
FAMILIES**

hundred Ranid species and more than three hundred Bufonids.

In everyday life, how can you tell frogs and toads apart? The typical frog is sleeker and faster than its toad cousin, has smoother skin, longer hind legs, jumps higher, and is generally found closer to water.

Toads, on the other hand, are short and squat, have dry, "warty" skin, short legs, and hop rather than jump. The drier, tougher, more waterproof skin allows them to live in habitats that are farther from water than most frogs. However, most toads must still return to the water to breed.

Frog Tales

While frogs have traditionally been popular characters in stories and folktales, they have not always been cast in a favorable light. This passage from the Grimm brothers' "The Frog Prince," first published in 1815, describes the transformation of the frog prince from an ugly frog into a handsome and heroic prince:

> . . . *But when the princess awoke on the following morning, she was astonished to see, instead of a frog, a handsome prince gazing on her with the most beautiful eyes that ever were seen, and standing at the head of her bed.*

However, among some ancient cultures, frogs were worshipped as gods. The ancient Egyptians, for example, believed that the frog-headed goddess Heket was one of the creators of the world. Many Egyptian kings were buried with mummified frogs to join them in their journey to the other world.

One of the most famous stories about frogs from ancient times appears in the Old Testament of the Bible. In the Book of Exodus, a plague of frogs swarmed from the rivers and invaded all the houses of Egypt.

In China and India, people thought the earth rested on the back of a giant frog. When this frog shook, earthquakes were felt all over the world. In China, instead of seeing a "man in the moon," people saw "a frog in the moon."

Many cultures viewed frogs as bringers of rain: the Mayan rain god Chac was a frog; the Indian Sanskrit word for frog means "cloud." And Native Americans correctly determined that listening to frog calls could help them predict the weather.

However, European cultures associated frogs, and especially toads, with evil and black magic. Witches were said to use toads in their recipes for magic potions and evil brews. The appearance of a toad was considered "evidence" that could help convict a suspect of witchcraft.

Gradually attitudes changed. In stories such as "The Frog Prince" and the Russian folktale "King of the Toads," frogs and toads were thought to be ugly and disgusting, but not evil.

By the late twentieth century, opinions about frogs and toads had come full circle. Today, you see them almost everywhere—on T-shirts, posters, and baseball caps, on television and as stuffed animals. One store, the Frog Museum in Eureka Springs, Arkansas, boasts over six thousand different frog items. That's more items than there are frog species in the entire world!

In literature, classic frog books include (among many) Beatrix Potter's *The Tale of Mr. Jeremy Fisher*, Arnold Lobel's Frog and Toad series, and Kenneth Grahame's *The Wind in the Willows*.

Clearly, frogs have come of age in today's world. This is a remarkable turn of events, especially when you consider that frogs are neither cuddly nor responsive to people. But the success of frogs in their own world has never depended on their loving nature. Rather, it is a story about survival in an uncertain and often hostile environment, a story that began some 230 million years ago, just after the height of what is known as the Age of Amphibians.

2 Frogs Through Time

THE CLEVER MEN AT OXFORD
KNOW ALL THAT THERE IS TO BE KNOWED
BUT THEY NONE OF THEM KNOW ONE HALF AS MUCH
AS INTELLIGENT MR. TOAD!

from *The Wind in the Willows*, Kenneth Grahame

As Earth's climate became warmer and drier, the lakes dried up. What had once been a shallow shoreline was now a patchwork of puddles. Many fish were left stranded, trapped in dead-end pools only a few inches deep. But one type of fish was different from the others. Its fins were stronger. It could maneuver through the mud from one puddle to the next. It could even use some of the oxygen from the air. In short, this new kind of fish had taken the first evolutionary step toward living on both land and water.

FOSSIL EVIDENCE SHOWS THAT THE BASIC FORM OF THE FROG HAS NOT CHANGED FOR MILLIONS OF YEARS.

Life began on Earth some 3.5 billion years ago. Bacteria and other single-celled organisms dominated the planet for the next 2.75 billion years. Then, around 750 million years ago, larger multicellular organisms began to appear, including the first vertebrates, the fishes. By the late Devonian period, some 365 million years ago, the seas were teeming with life, but the land around them remained relatively barren. Only a few plants and invertebrates had made the move from the water onto land.

During the late Devonian the planet went through repeated cycles of rain and drought. Shallow lakes formed on the land, then quickly dried up. Fishes and other creatures were left stranded in the hot sun. Most of them died, but a few struggled through the mud in this harsh new environment, gasping for oxygen.

The result of these environmental changes was the emergence of two new kinds of fish that were the forerunners of amphibians. The lobed-finned fish and the lungfish had developed adaptations that allowed them to survive for periods of time outside of the water.

The lobe-fins had special "fingerlike" fins that resembled primitive legs and could be used for locomotion during periods when the lobe-fins were left stranded in the mud. Lungfish, on the other hand, developed a different but equally useful adaption for terrestrial life: lungs.

Early Amphibians

Which creature gave rise to the first amphibian—the lobe-fin or the lungfish? Biologists remain divided over the answer. Body structure and evidence from developing eggs point to the lobe-fins as being the direct link to the first amphibians. Fossil evidence, on the other hand, favors the lungfish.

FOSSILS

How do we know what we know about evolution? Much of our information comes from fossils, the remains of once-living organisms. In most cases, fossils preserve the hard parts of organisms such as their bones, shells, or teeth.

Preservation takes place in different ways. Some fossils are simply imprints of bodies that once existed but are now gone. A footprint in stone can be a fossil. So can the outline of a creature that was buried in sand. Under some conditions, rocklike minerals slowly replace the body tissues of an organism. Over thousands of years, these minerals form a fossil that is petrified, or turned to stone.

The value of fossils to evolutionary scientists is enormous. What fossils show is the progression of different organism types through time. Fossils from Precambrian rocks (more than 600 million years old) show tiny, simple organisms. Large organisms with hard shells begin to appear about 600 million years ago. As time passes, more and more complicated organisms appear, such as fish, insects, and finally, the amphibian ancestors of frogs.

When looking at a fossil record it is important to remember that it presents a kind of calendar of the past from which you can determine dates. Thus, you will not find a single amphibian fossil in rocks that are more than 365 million years old. On the other hand, amphibians are quite common in rocks that are less than 365 million years old. This is why scientists conclude that amphibians evolved about 365 million years ago—before that time you don't see them; after that time they are abundant.

ONLY THE HARD PARTS OF THIS SPADEFOOT TOAD WERE PRESERVED AS A FOSSIL.

In any case, biologists agree that the first amphibians moved to land about 365 million years ago. Now that they were out of the water, the early amphibians were completely out of reach of their water-bound former predators. They also enjoyed the rich new food supply awaiting them on land. But in order to take full advantage of this new territory, these early amphibians had some critical problems to solve.

Staying Wet. Water is perhaps the most vital substance for living things. About 70 percent of most land organisms, including your own body, is composed of water. All chemical reactions take place in it.

Maintaining body water is ordinarily not a problem for aquatic organisms—whatever water they lose is quickly replaced. Terrestrial organisms, on the other hand, lose significant amounts of water through evaporation. Lost water is replaced either by drinking, eating, or by taking in water through the skin.

An impermeable, or waterproof, outer skin decreases water loss for many terrestrial vertebrates, such as reptiles, birds, and mammals. But amphibian skin, which is used as a respiratory organ, must stay wet and permeable (porous) at all times to allow gases to diffuse in and out. For this reason, amphibians had to stay close to water.

Frogs take in water in a variety of ways. Some frogs dive into the water every few minutes to keep themselves wet. Other frogs live in humid habitats that keep their skin wet at all times. Many toads have baggy "seats" under their legs that absorb water from a shallow pool. Still other frogs and toads burrow underground or build cocoons to retain the water they already have.

The only method of hydration, or taking in water, that most frogs don't use is drinking by mouth. Out of about 3,500 different frog species, only one frog, the painted-belly monkey, is known to

MANY FROGS NEVER VENTURE FAR FROM THE WATER.

drink through its mouth! The rest get their water some other way.

Breathing. In the same way that fire uses oxygen to burn wood and release energy, organisms obtain energy by burning, or oxidizing, the food they eat. This process of combining oxygen with food to obtain food energy is called respiration, or breathing.

Every multicellular animal must carry out respiration. Gills provide a thin membrane through which oxygen can diffuse inward and carbon dioxide can diffuse outward. Gills are located on the outside of the body so they can absorb oxygen directly from the surrounding water.

Gills work very efficiently underwater. But they need to stay wet. When they are exposed to the air, gills lose water so quickly that they collapse. The animal loses its ability to exchange oxygen and carbon dioxide. To keep their respiratory surfaces from drying out, the first amphibians developed a set of "interior gills," otherwise known as lungs.

Lungs function much like gills, but they are located inside the body and encased in a protective covering to prevent dehydration. Amphibians were the first land animals to develop them. Compared to the lungs of reptiles or mammals, amphibian lungs are not very efficient. For this reason, amphibians developed a second respiratory medium in their skin. But their skin, like any other respiratory organ, had to stay wet. Amphibians accomplished this by living in moist environments and by developing glands to secrete mucus to keep their skin from drying out.

Moving Around. Living on land is harder work than living in water. If you don't believe this, try lifting a heavy object underwater. The water helps support the object, making it seem much lighter than it would in the air. This buoyancy of objects in water allowed aquatic organisms to grow to very large sizes without having much body support.

Without water, terrestrial animals needed stronger support to function on land. Arthropods such as insects solved the support problem by developing strong exoskeletons, hard skeletons on the outer surface of the body. Amphibians solved the support problem in a different way. They developed strong internal vertebral columns (backbones) with an arch. This arch, much like a bridge, allowed weight from each side to push toward the center.

For movement, amphibians faced a whole new set of problems. In the water, they simply glided by pushing against the surrounding medium with their fins. On land, the surrounding medium, air, is too thin to push against. So amphibians evolved a different strategy. They developed strong legs and feet that could move independently from their backbones and push off the ground to propel themselves ahead. Amphibians were the first vertebrates to have legs and feet. The five-toed design of the

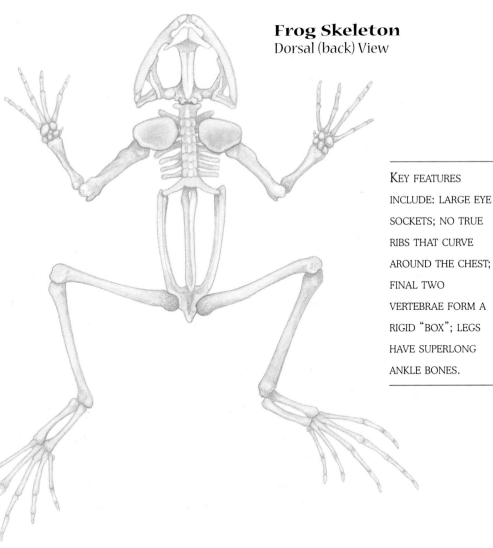

Frog Skeleton
Dorsal (back) View

KEY FEATURES INCLUDE: LARGE EYE SOCKETS; NO TRUE RIBS THAT CURVE AROUND THE CHEST; FINAL TWO VERTEBRAE FORM A RIGID "BOX"; LEGS HAVE SUPERLONG ANKLE BONES.

early amphibians is retained in organisms as varied as bats, whales, and humans.

Reproducing. In reproduction, amphibians faced perhaps the most difficult problem of all. Where should they lay their eggs? If they laid them on land, the eggs would dry up long before they were ready to hatch. If they laid their eggs underwater, the hatchlings would start out life in a hostile environment in which they could not even draw a first breath of air!

The problem was solved by a kind of compromise. Frogs and other amphibians returned to the water to lay eggs. But when the eggs hatched, they started out life not as air-breathing terrestrial animals but as larvae (immature forms of the organism) that breathe through fishlike gills.

Newborn amphibians have more in common with fish than they do with most land animals. Tadpoles (frog larvae) have long tails, no arms or legs, and breathe through gills instead of lungs. As they grow, they go through an amazing process called metamorphosis, in which their body form changes. During metamorphosis, tadpoles gradually become more froglike, losing their tails, growing limbs, and developing internal lungs for living life on land.

Sensing the World. Information travels differently in air than it does in water. Sound, for example, seems distorted to us when we hear things underwater because our sensory organs are designed to work on land, through the medium of air. The first amphibians had the opposite problem: because their hearing organs were designed to work in water, sound traveling through air seemed distorted.

In the move from water to land, vision and sound were perhaps the most strongly distorted. For vision, frogs developed a nictitating membrane, which could be pulled down like a window shade to protect the eyes when the organism went underwater. For sensing sound, amphibians developed a new type of ear.

Sound is the result of vibrations. In fish and other aquatic organisms, sound vibrations disturb a pool of water located on the outside of the organism's body. This disturbance stimulates the nerve endings to send messages to the brain.

The amphibian ear also uses sound vibrations in water to stimulate nerve endings. But the water is located inside the body. Vibrations from an outer eardrum disturb a small pool of water in the inner ear, stimulating nerve endings to send messages to the brain. Your own ears work in much this way.

Frog Fossils

One by one, amphibians solved these problems and moved onto land. They kept wet, obtained oxygen, developed legs and a strong skeleton, gained the ability to reproduce by going through metamorphosis, and developed new sensory organs that functioned on land.

Over time, the amphibians became a very successful terrestrial group. During the Carboniferous period (363 to 290 million years ago) they dominated the earth. This time has often been called the Age of Amphibians. Many Carboniferous amphibians grew to lengths of 13 feet (4 m) or more, in many ways resembling the reptiles during the Age of Dinosaurs.

The oldest known amphibian fossil is *Ichthyostega*, which lived about 350 million years ago. The crocodile-like *Eryops* was an amphibian that lived during the Permian period, the height of the Age of Amphibians, about 260 million years ago. By the beginning of the Triassic period, most large amphibians had died out. They could not compete with the even larger—and fully terrestrial—reptiles, which were beginning to proliferate.

Frog Evolution

ERA	Precambrian				Paleozoic	
PERIOD		Cambrian	Ordovician	Silurian	Devonian	
millions of years ago	570	510	439	409	363	

365
first
amphibians

It was after the very large amphibians had already died out that *Triadobatrachus*, the oldest known fossil frog, lived in Madagascar, about 220 to 230 million years ago. *Triadobatrachus* was either an aquatic frog or a tadpole undergoing metamorphosis.

In any event, some 50 to 60 million years passed until the next recognizable frog showed up in the fossil record. By then, frogs had come to resemble the Discoglossid frogs that live today.

The oldest fossil frogs date back to the period when Earth had two major supercontinents, Laurasia and Gondwanaland. No descendants of these frogs are believed to be alive today.

The oldest living frog groups are the Leiopelmatidae and Disglossidae, which date back 150 million years or more, to the Jurassic period. During the Jurassic, all of Earth's landmasses were combined in a single supercontinent called Pangaea.

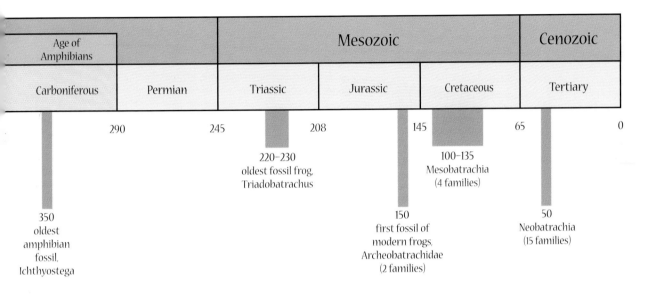

Scientists think that all modern frogs arose and dispersed all over Pangaea during this time, eventually becoming separated when Pangaea broke up into separate continents.

The twenty-one frog families are divided into three large groups. Together, the Leiopelmatidae and Disglossidae are called the Archaeobactridae, or most ancient group. The Mesobatrachia includes four frog families of medium age, dating back 100 to 135 million years. The remaining fifteen frog families comprise the Neobatrachia and date back 50 million years or less.

Here are members of seven different frog families—a glimpse of the tremendous variety within the world of frogs. Their family name, in Latin, is followed by their common species name.

Centrolenidae: glass frog

Discoglossidae: Oriental fire-bellied toad

Dendrobatidae: blue poison dart frog

Pelobatidae: plains spadefoot toad

Ranidae: southern leopard frog

Hylidae: masked tree frog

Leptodactylidae: Cranwell's horned frog

3

The Frog, Inside and Out

> EACH [FROG] REPRESENTS A HIGH SPECIALIZATION ALONG A GIVEN LINE OF DEVELOPMENT, AND SEEMS PERFECTED TO THE MINUTEST DETAIL IN ITS FITNESS FOR ITS LIFE.
>
> from "The Frog Book," Mary Dickerson, 1906

At midday, the bullfrog sits at the edge of the pond. It has been gorging itself on insects all morning. Suddenly, a disturbance enters its field of vision: a dog. The dog slowly comes closer. Is it a danger? The frog doesn't wait to find out. Nerve impulses from the frog's brain send a message to its legs: *jump!*

An instant later, the frog's long hind legs begin to unfold. Working like powerful levers, they propel the frog far into the air. In mid jump, the frog's body flattens to a sleek aerodynamic shape, guiding it to the splashdown. With a distinct *plop!* the frog enters the water several feet away from its would-be predator and swims off.

A LEOPARD FROG RISES OUT OF THE WATER.

Body Plan: Exterior

The plan for the frog's body took shape about 150 million years ago when ancient relatives of the Leiopelmatidae (tailed frogs) first appeared. Frogs vary widely in shape, but most follow the same basic design.

A biologist can identify frog species by noting differences among characteristics such as the shape of the frog's pupil, the length of its leg bones, and the size and shape of its feet. Generally speaking, a frog's shape, color, and physical features provide valuable clues about lifestyle and habitat. Thus, the web-footed African clawed frog with its smooth, flattened body

Leopard Frog Body

lives in an aquatic habitat and uses its wide, oversized, hind webbed feet for swimming. The spadefoot toad, on the other hand, lives in arid regions and uses its bony, shovel-like back legs to dig backward into the soil and hide from predators.

Frogs that hide in their habitat to escape being noticed by predators tend to be stout, stumpy, and dull colored with short hind legs, such as the American toad. Frogs that need to leap to escape predators tend to have sleek bodies and very long hind legs, such as the pond-dwelling pickerel frog. The telltale features of a tree frog are the long digits on the ends of the feet equipped with disklike suction cups for gripping slippery tree surfaces.

Body Plan: Interior

The skeletal design of frogs hinges on simplicity. In fact, frogs have fewer bones than other vertebrates, including their closest evolutionary relatives, fishes and reptiles. The frog skeleton is characterized by a short spine, an absence of ribs, and elongated leg bones, especially in the ankle. This basic design has served frogs well; with few changes frogs have been able to adapt to living on land, in trees, underground, and underwater.

The internal anatomy of a frog is also simple. The digestive, urinary, and reproductive systems all empty into a single opening, the cloaca. Amphibians were the first vertebrates to feature a heart with three chambers—a major advance over the two-chambered designs of fishes. In two-chambered hearts, with each heartbeat, the blood flow slows down and blood pressure drops.

Three-chambered hearts have two separate blood circuits. One circuit goes to the lungs. The other circuit takes the blood that has returned from the lungs and pumps it to the rest of the body at high pressure. This increased blood pressure allows amphibians to be more active than organisms with two-chambered

Frog Organs
Ventral (underside) View

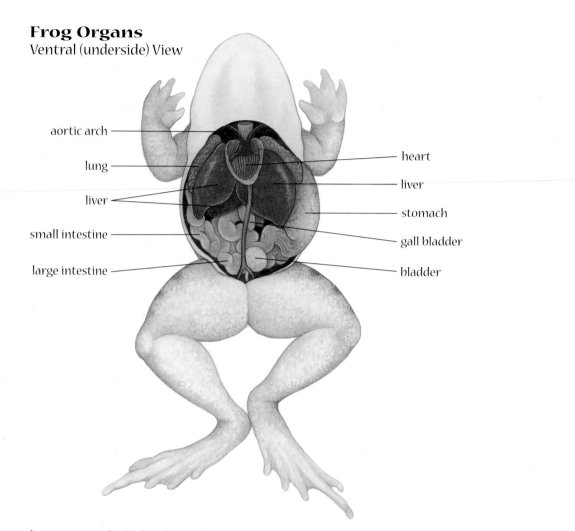

aortic arch

lung

liver

small intestine

large intestine

heart

liver

stomach

gall bladder

bladder

hearts, as their body cells are replenished more quickly with fresh blood than the cells of their two-chambered counterparts.

Skin

The skin is perhaps the most noticeable characteristic of frogs and toads. Skin may be smooth or rough, blotchy, striped, banded, bumpy, speckled, spotted, and just about everything in between. Colors range from dull green and gray to a spectacular array of high contrast reds, blues, yellows, purples, and oranges.

The function of a frog's skin is to offer protection as well as a wet medium in which the exchange, or diffusion, of oxygen and carbon dioxide can take place. To keep their skin wet, frogs secrete a mucus coating over the skin through special glands.

Other skin glands secrete poisons ranging from the mildly distasteful in some frog species to the deadly toxic poison given off by *Phyllobates terribilis*, a South American poison dart frog. The toxin from one member of this species is potent enough to kill 10 adult human beings or 20,000 laboratory mice!

Surprisingly, few predators are victimized by this poison. What makes them stay away? Poison dart frogs and other highly toxic frogs display bright coloration—a warning not to attack.

These bright colors ward off predators so well that some nonpoisonous frogs avoid being eaten by mimicking the colors of poisonous species. For example, the skin of the nonpoisonous

AS TADPOLES, POISON DART FROGS ARE DULL IN COLOR AND NOT VERY TOXIC. WHEN THEY MATURE, THE BRIGHT COLOR APPEARS, A SIGN THE TOXINS IN THEIR SKIN HAVE INCREASED TO FULL STRENGTH.

Fort Randolph robber frog closely resembles the color pattern of the highly toxic lovely poison dart frog. Potential predators assume the robber frog is poisonous too.

Unlike poison dart frogs, most nonpoisonous frogs seek to go *unnoticed* rather than noticed by predators. They become inconspicuous by camouflaging themselves, using colors and patterns to blend into a background. The horned toad, for example, has flat, mottled skin that blends perfectly with dried leaves. A panther toad, on the other hand, has skin that matches tree bark. Many frogs have a dark or bright line on their back to break up their profile so it will not resemble the shape of an anuran. Other

BLENDING IN. RIDGES ON THE MALAYSIAN HORNED FROG LOOK LIKE THE EDGES OF DEAD LEAVES.

frogs can change color from dark to light or green to brown.

Some people think that frogs change color to camouflage themselves in changing backgrounds. However, most research shows that color change in frogs is actually dependent on temperature, light, humidity, and stress rather than the color of their environment.

Color Up Close

Color in frog skin is created in a remarkable way. Frog skin is studded with three types of pigment cells. Melanophores contain dark pigments: black, brown, or red. Xanthophores give rise to yellows, oranges, and reds. Iridophores do not produce color but scatter light to produce blue—much in the same way that air molecules in the sky produce a blue color.

The color of the frog depends on whether the pigments are concentrated or dispersed. Cold or wet conditions cause the pigments to concentrate in bunches. This makes the frog appear light in color.

Warm and bright conditions cause the pigments to disperse, or spread out. This makes the frog appear dark in color. The colors themselves are brought about in combinations. For example, even bright green frogs do not have green pigment in their skin. Instead, green is produced by a combination of yellow xanthophores and blue iridophores. The yellow overlays the blue, producing the optical effect of green to the human eye.

Eyes

Herpetologist H. Rucker Smyth describes frog eyes as "undoubtedly the most beautiful eyes in the Animal Kingdom." Frog eyes come in a variety of shapes and colors—gold, silver, bronze,

MOST FROGS IN THE UNITED STATES HAVE EYES WITH HORIZONTAL PUPILS, WHICH
HELP THEM SEE IN LOW LIGHT.

copper, as well as strikingly vivid reds, oranges, yellows, and blues.

Pupils are typically horizontal in the Ranidae ("true" frog), Bufonidae (toad), and Dendrobatidae families (poison dart frogs) and vertical in the spadefoot toad family (Pelobatidae) and Lepto-dactylidae family. Other shapes, including round and heart-shaped pupils, also occur.

Most frogs that hunt have remarkably large and luminous eyes. The red-eyed tree frog, for example, has huge eyes for its size that dilate at night when it is active to take in more light.

One thing frogs can't do is move their eyes to see an object. Instead, frogs have to move their entire head to view something that is beyond their field of vision. Fortunately, most frogs have an incredibly wide field of vision that extends all the way around and even behind their body. This is one reason why it is so hard to sneak up on a frog—it can literally see in back of its head!

Ears

Frog ears are modest things. Many vertebrates (such as human beings) have ears that stick out. Frog ears, on the other hand, blend with the frog's overall streamlined design. Nevertheless, hearing plays a critical role in a frog's life. The songs and croaking choruses performed by the males of many species can be fully appreciated only by ears that are designed to hear them. In fact, there is evidence that frogs' hearing may be "tuned" to hear mating calls from frogs of their own species and little else.

Hearing is also an important part of the frog's system of self-defense. Even so, H. Rucker Smyth thinks that hearing serves mainly to alert a frog rather than to initiate action. "A sudden loud noise will startle a human being into action," Smyth says, "but the same noise merely puts an amphibian on guard and ready to flee. It seems to require vision to fully interpret the sounds it hears."

Legs

The all-time leaping record set by a frog measured an astounding 17.5 feet (5.3 m) on a single jump. This record was accomplished by a mascarene frog, which also jumped 33.5 feet (10.2 m) in a series of three consecutive jumps. Smaller frogs can also be champion leapers, such as the green tree frog of North America, a 2.5-inch (6.35-cm) frog that jumps up to 10 feet (3.0 m). That's 48 times its body length!

Not all frogs are great jumpers. Many toads, for example, and burrowing frogs have short hind legs and hop rather than leap. Nevertheless, all frogs are capable of some kind of leaping

HOW FROGS LEAP

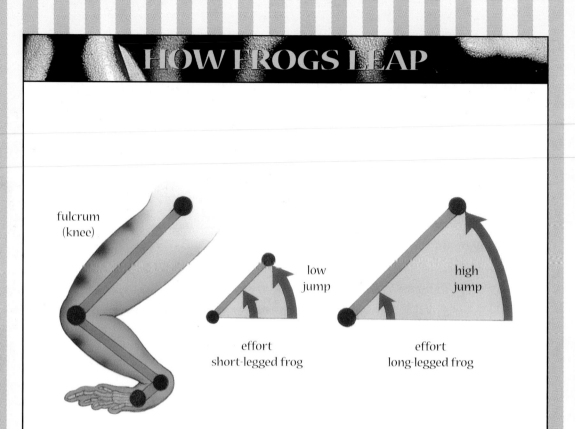

fulcrum
(knee)

low
jump

effort
short-legged frog

high
jump

effort
long-legged frog

ow does the frog get such power into its leap? Longer legs provide more height for the same force than shorter legs do. The frog's leg works as a series of levers. Focusing on just one of the levers shows how extra length can result in extra jump height.

Take a look at the lever. It works like a hinge. Both short- and long-legged frogs use muscle power to move their legs. The part of the leg near the hinge moves the same distance in both frogs. But the end of the leg moves much farther in the long-legged frog, producing a much higher jump.

THE STICKY DISKS ON THE FEET OF THIS EUROPEAN TREE FROG HELP IT CLING TO A BRANCH WHEN IT LANDS.

motion in which both hind legs push off the ground with a great deal of lift and force.

How are frogs able to make such prodigious leaps? In general, the longer a frog's hind legs are, the better a leaper it will be. The frog's hind leg bones are more elongated than those of other mammals, especially in the lower leg and ankle area. The elongated ankle gives frogs extra bone length that can produce extra leverage in a jump.

Is there a perfect frog body? Many species fit the classic image of the frog as smooth, sleek, and powerful. In a sense, however, every frog is perfect for the lifestyle it leads and the environment in which it lives. Some frogs are streamlined; others are stumpy and squat. But all frogs are designed to function efficiently in the habitat in which they spend their lives.

4 Frog Ways

> FROGS DO FOR THE NIGHT WHAT BIRDS DO FOR
> THE DAY: THEY GIVE IT A VOICE.
>
> Archie Carr, author, naturalist, and herpetologist

During the day, the green tree frog stays fairly quiet among the leaves. But when dusk arrives during breeding season, the concert begins. As the male frogs approach their breeding ponds, they begin to emit their territorial calls: *quank! quank! quank!*

These calls tell other males to back off—*this territory is taken!* As time passes, the males space themselves out around the ponds. Now it's time for the full concert—as many as one hundred frogs chime in with their courtship call: *bo bape, bo bape, bo bape!* The noise that results, according to noted frog

MARSH MUSIC. ONLY MALE FROGS HAVE
VOCAL SACS FOR MAKING CALLS.

authorities Pete Carmichael and Winston Williams, "is nothing short of mind-boggling."

Frog Songs

Frogs display a rich range of behaviors—from hunting and feeding, to protecting themselves, to mating and reproducing. But no aspect of frog behavior is more fascinating than the way frogs communicate through song.

Frog songs are truly one of the wonders of nature—according to paleontologist Robert Bakker, "the richest sonic symphonies in today's ecosystem." They were also the first true songs created by vocal cords, preceding the songs of birds by millions of years. (Insect songs, such as the chirping of a cricket, are created not with vocal cords but by rubbing together body surfaces.) Frog songs range from the lonely solo of a bullfrog to the din created by a chorus of tree frogs so loud that medieval nobles employed servants to "beat the pond" for the purpose of disturbing the frogs and breaking up their concert.

Are frogs simply making noise or are they making music? The answer is neither. Frog songs are a form of communication.

Making the Call. Frog calls come in an amazing variety. Each species sings its own songs. And within a species, different calls have different meanings. Thus, the whistles, warbles, woofs, croaks, grunts, squeaks, squawks, chuckles, clicks, and pops are all meant to convey information.

What is it that frogs are trying to communicate through their songs? First and foremost, the singers want to announce that they are ready to mate. Other messages convey that frogs are entering each other's territory, that they are ready to fight, that they do *not* want to mate, and finally, that they sense danger or are in distress.

Typically, frog calls occur after nightfall and are emitted by males rather than females (though females in a few species sing out responses to a male's call). In general, smaller species (and smaller frogs within a species) make higher-pitched calls.

To make a call, the frog first draws in air to fill its vocal sacs. Each vocal sac bulges outward like an inflated balloon. Then the air in the sac is pumped back and forth, from the sac to the lungs and back, making a different sound each time it passes over the changing shape of the vocal cords.

CHANGING THEIR TUNE. SOME FROG SPECIES SING A TERRITORIAL SONG AT DUSK TO WARD OFF RIVAL MALES. LATER, THE SAME FROGS WILL ATTRACT FEMALES WITH MATING SONGS.

Calls are grouped in four categories. The advertisement call, formerly known as the mating call, comes in three forms: the courtship call, the territorial call, and the encounter call. The courtship call advertises that a male wants to attract females. The territorial call announces to rival males that a male is making a claim on a territory. An encounter call occurs when two males enter the same territory. Usually the smaller male backs off, but sometimes the encounter results in wrestling, butting, or some type of fighting.

Other calls include reciprocation calls from females to males (emitted by only a few species, including the midwife toad and members of the Leptodactylid family), release calls for unsuccessful matings to stop, and distress calls, sent out as alarms when predators enter an area.

Anural Tunes. Each frog call has its own pattern, tune, or pitch. Some calls are simply monotonous repetitions of a single note. Others can be complex and melodious arrangements of notes and chords, rivaling birdsong in richness and musical quality.

Songs tend to be more sophisticated when more than one species is located in the same area. In that case, species need to identify themselves so they don't end up attracting a member of the "wrong" species. In contrast, songs of frog species that are the sole inhabitants of breeding grounds tend to be simple and repetitious. In fact, a few frog species attract a mate without making calls of any kind.

Frog biologists suspect that larger males with deeper, louder advertising calls tend to be chosen by females more frequently than smaller, high-pitched males of the same species. More data will need to be collected before this hypothesis is fully verified. In any event, advertising calls vary greatly. Some of the more notable calls include the pig frog that grunts like a barnyard pig, the barking tree frog that woofs like a dog, and the carpenter frog that makes sounds like carpenters hammering nails.

Why Songs? Almost all frogs produce some kind of singing, yet few members of their closest amphibian relatives, the salamanders, produce any kind of vocalization. This poses a more general question: Why do frogs sing at all? Biologists William Duellman and Linda Trueb suggest that singing animals are those that leap or fly, such as cicadas and crickets, and cannot be tracked by smell. Almost all birds sing because their flight makes them difficult to locate using other senses. Similarly, the highly vocal mammals include bats and primates, which fly or swing through the trees in discontinuous leaps.

Frogs, as leapers, share this trait of taking discontinuous leaps over the landscape. For animals that rely on smell, these leaps make frogs all but untrackable. In order to make themselves available again, frogs use songs so that members of the same species can find one another.

Defense

For frogs, the world is a dangerous place. Unlike many other vertebrates, frogs do not possess sharp teeth, claws, horns, or any other defensive weapons. As if a lack of weaponry weren't enough of a handicap, frogs also spend part of each day making conspicuous vocal calls that, while they may successfully attract the attention of a mate, also attract the attention of predators.

And what a variety of predators frogs have! Animals that eat frogs include birds, such as herons and storks; fish, which eat both tadpoles and frog eggs as well as adult frogs; reptiles, such as turtles and alligators; and mammals, such as shrews and raccoons.

With such an array of hungry foes, it is a wonder that any frogs at all survive to adulthood. In fact, few frog eggs actually

OUT IN THE OPEN. FROGS HAVE FEW DEFENSES AGAINST A DETERMINED ENEMY.

do reach maturity; a study of cane toads shows that as few as 1 in 200 eggs (0.5 percent) make it to reproductive age. Even at this rate, cane toad populations still stand a good chance of increasing, because a female cane toad lays up to 35,000 eggs at a time! This ability to lay enormous numbers of eggs is ultimately the frog's most effective defense strategy. A small fraction of individuals may survive, but if there are enough individuals, the population will increase.

Fight or Flight? While frogs lack offensive weaponry, they are not without a sophisticated battery of defenses. The first line of defense for most frogs is to be inconspicuous. Within their habitats, frogs hide in a variety of clever places, including under rocks, between leaves, inside dark crevices, or buried in rubble or soil. Indeed, biologist Mary Dickerson says, "Each [frog] is so invisible in its environment that it seems wonderful that an enemy ever finds it at all."

Camouflage helps immensely. It is no surprise that almost all frogs are closely matched in color and pattern to their habitat. Thus, frogs that live among leaves and algae are green; frogs that live among dead leaves on forest floors tend to be brown; and frogs that live in sandy habitats are apt to be yellow. Any visual trick that prevents a would-be predator from recognizing

PREDATORS LOOK FOR THE CLEAR OUTLINE OF A FROG. COLORS THAT BLEND WITH THE BACKGROUND OR MARKINGS THAT BREAK UP THE FORM WILL CONFUSE AN ENEMY.

the frog's familiar profile may be a lifesaver. Stripes, bars, shadings, lines, false eyeballs, and other deceptive markings all help to fool enemies and so allow frogs an escape.

Once frogs are recognized, they reach deeper into their bag of defensive tricks. For many frog species, flight is the best option. Frogs such as the leopard frog, mascarene frog, and Southern cricket frog, are superb leapers, capable of evading enemies at a single bound. Tree frogs, with their long toes and sticky disks, acrobatically swing and dangle from branch to branch and leaf to leaf to avoid capture. The flying frogs of Malaysia, Japan, and other parts of Asia will jump out of trees to what seems like certain destruction, only to spread out their winglike 10-inch (6-cm) webbed legs and glide to safety.

At the point of recognition, some leapers such as the green tree frog surprise the enemy during their jump by exposing shockingly bright colors on the undersides of their bodies. This sudden flash of brilliance may confuse or disorient predators for the split second it takes for the frog to get away.

Not all frogs are great leapers. Many nonleapers such as the Eurasian toad defend themselves by puffing up their bodies to look bigger than they usually are. Other frogs use different methods of bluff and intimidation. Fire-bellied toads expose their fiery undersides to startle foes, while some tree frogs achieve the same effect using a bright orange tongue. Budgett's frog from Argentina goes through an entire routine of gaping, bellowing, screaming, and grunting to scare off attackers.

The Final Defense. When all else fails, an effective tactic for many frog species is to play dead. Predators, in most cases, are interested in live prey, so pretending to be limp and lifeless can cause a hungry enemy to lose interest.

In some cases, nothing works. The frog tries to hide, escape, startle, jump, swim, play dead, or scare its way to safety but the

THE BRIGHT COLORS OF THE ORIENTAL FIRE-BELLIED TOAD ARE JUST ENOUGH OF A
DISTRACTION TO CAUSE A PREDATOR TO MISS ITS PREY.

enemy persists and takes the frog into its mouth. It is here that
the frog's final layer of protection comes into play: poison.

Some toxins, like those present in the pickerel frog, are
merely bad-tasting and discourage such predators as garter
snakes from even putting a pickerel frog into their mouths.
Others, like the toxin from the Colorado river toad, are secreted
as a milky white liquid from the parotoid gland between the eyes
and can have a more serious effect on predators. While few

POISON DART FROGS ARE SOCIAL CREATURES THAT LIVE IN GROUPS. WHEN THESE
FROGS ARE BRED IN CAPTIVITY, THEIR POISON LOSES MUCH OF ITS POTENCY.

North American frog species pose a threat to human beings, biologists advise people to wash their hands after they handle most frogs, especially toads (which tend to have more potent toxins).

The most famous toxins of all belong to the *Dendrobates* and *Phyllobates* poison dart frogs of Central and South America. Poisons from these frogs can kill almost any predator unwise enough to take them in. The brilliant coloration of the poison dart frogs warns predators to *stay away!* For the most part, the warnings are heeded. Poison dart frogs live a remarkably carefree life in which they move conspicuously through their habitat, confident that most predators won't dare go near them.

In fact, poison dart frogs have only two known predators— a frog-eating snake immune to its toxin, and human beings. The Choco Indians of South America use the toxins from poison dart frogs to tip their hunting arrows. In some cases the hunters need to kill the frogs to extract the poison. However, toxin from the most potent of them can be gathered simply by passing a dart across the animal's back.

Hunting

All adult frogs are carnivores that eat live prey. Tadpoles, on the other hand, are almost exclusively herbivores (plant-eaters). Frog food sources vary widely, depending on the species and habitat. Generally, frogs are voracious eaters that will attack any prey of the appropriate size—ants, flies, beetles, worms, termites, slugs, snails, and other invertebrates. Larger frog species may prey on small rodents and the young of birds, snakes, and other vertebrates. One African bullfrog, for example, was found in the snake cage of a zoo having eaten sixteen young ringhals cobra snakes and about to finish off its seventeenth!

Feeding data is hard to come by for most frog species. One

THIS CHACO HORNED FROG IS EATING A YOUNG CAIMAN. FOR EXTRA CHEWING FORCE, HORNED FROGS USE THEIR EYEBALL MUSCLES TO APPLY PRESSURE TO CAPTURED PREY.

study estimates that one species of tree frog consumes about twenty prey per day. Observations suggest that many frogs consume much more. For example, the cane toad has been observed in front of a beehive, intercepting one bee after another as the workers returned to their hive.

Hunting strategies vary according to species. Frogs that eat such things as termites and ants tend to seek out their prey where it lives. More familiar pond frogs have been described as "opportunistic" eaters: they sit quietly in a likely spot and strike at any prey of the appropriate size within their range.

The most common method of food capture is the tongue flip. Like a guided missile, the frog launches an all-out attack, often jumping a considerable distance as it extends its tongue at the target. To be successful, the frog must judge distance and movement with precision.

FREEZE! THE BEST WAY TO AVOID BECOMING A FROG'S PREY IS NOT TO MOVE AT ALL.

Here is the typical sequence of events in an attack: a European common frog sits quietly on a rock, surveying the scene. Its stillness and camouflage help it blend with its surroundings, to the point where it is almost invisible to potential prey. The frog does not respond to most visual stimuli, such as a branch swaying in the breeze or a bird flying high overhead. However, when an object of the appropriate size such as a beetle enters its field of vision, it is alerted.

For a few seconds, the frog sizes up its prey. If the prey stops moving for an extended period of time, the frog may lose interest. However, if the prey shows the slightest twitch of movement, the frog attacks, leaping at its prey as its long tongue unfolds. The tongue is coated with sticky mucus, so that any kind of contact usually results in capture. The tongue folds back in the blink of an eye, bringing the prey into the mouth at lightning-fast speed. The encounter ends as the frog presses the prey against the roof of its mouth and swallows it whole.

Temperature and Moisture Control

Two factors above everything else influence a frog's behavior: temperature and moisture. As ectotherms, frogs need to obtain warmth from the outside environment to raise their body temperature. However, most frogs cannot bask in the sun as reptiles do without drying out their skin. For this reason, frogs tend to be found exclusively in environments that are both warm *and* wet.

Typically, frogs function best at temperatures between 68° and 86° Fahrenheit (20°–30° C). This matches the temperature

---

A BULLFROG'S TONGUE FLIP

range of the tropical habitats where the majority of frog species are found. When the temperature drops below 68° F (20° C) the frog's body metabolism drops. Gray tree frogs and spring peepers can withstand temperatures that drop so far that 65 percent of their body turns to ice. They accomplish this by diluting

THE EASTERN SPADEFOOT TOAD WILL DIG BACKWARD TO ESCAPE AN ENEMY.

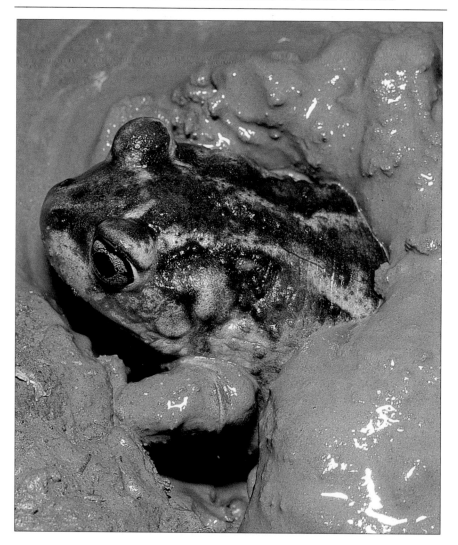

their blood with a form of "biological antifreeze"—glycerol, or high concentrations of blood sugar.

During prolonged periods of cold, many frogs that live in temperate climates hibernate. Toads typically hibernate by burrowing underground. Frogs take refuge in the mud at the bottom of ponds or in cracks, crevices, or other protected spots in their environment.

Spadefoot toads and other desert frogs undergo estivation —or heat hibernation—by burying themselves underground during periods of prolonged heat or dryness. Experiments show that any sign of moisture in the soil is enough to revive an estivating frog and induce it to come to the surface.

5 The Mating Game

> THE FROG POOL WAS SQUARE. . . . THERE WERE FROGS
> THERE ALL RIGHT, THOUSANDS OF THEM. THEIR VOICES
> BEAT THE NIGHT, THEY BOOMED AND BARKED AND
> CROAKED AND RATTLED. THEY SANG TO THE STARS, TO
> THE WANING MOON, TO THE WAVING GRASSES. THEY
> BELLOWED LOVE SONGS AND CHALLENGES.
>
> from *Cannery Row*, John Steinbeck

Tonight's the night. At the breeding pond, the croaking chorus of the wood frogs has reached a crescendo. The males are waiting. The females are finally starting to arrive. In their eagerness to mate, males will pounce on anything—a rock, a shoe, a fish, even another male frog. The more fortunate males latch onto females, whose egg-engorged bodies dwarf them in size. The less fortunate males grab onto something else; if it turns out to be another male they hear a sharp release call as it tries to shake free.

THE BASIC SCHEME OF FROG REPRODUCTION IS A SIMPLE SIX-STAGE process: In the spring, adult frogs come into a state of mating

THE SONG OF THE SPRING PEEPER HAS BEEN COMPARED
TO THE SOUND OF SLEIGH BELLS.

readiness. The males then sing their "love songs" to attract females to their breeding ponds. A female pairs up with a male in a process called amplexus. At the end of amplexus the male releases sperm over the eggs as the female deposits them into the water. The fertilized eggs grow and hatch into aquatic tadpoles. The tadpoles then go through the process of metamorphosis, emerging several weeks later as adult frogs.

Almost all frog species follow this six-stage plan. But few frogs adhere precisely to each step. In fact, with regard to reproduction, frogs have been called "the most diverse vertebrates on Earth."

The most common way for frogs to reproduce is to lay eggs in standing water. But frogs also lay their eggs on rocks and leaves and in trees high above the water; in roots, burrows, mud nests, and tree stumps. When the eggs hatch, many of them drop, roll, or wriggle into the water, to live the next stage as tadpoles.

Breeding Types

Frogs fall into two distinct categories—explosive breeders and prolonged breeders. Explosive breeders such as the wood frog, leopard frog, and spadefoot toad gather at a breeding site and engage in a mad, no-holds-barred, reproductive free-for-all. Prolonged breeders, such as the bullfrog, green frog, and most tree frogs, breed at a slower pace.

Explosive breeders tend to live in highly seasonal habitats in which winters are followed by heavy spring rains. These rains serve as the signal that stimulates explosive breeders to begin the breeding process. The rains create the temporary pools the frogs use as their breeding ponds.

The explosive breeding process is initiated as male frogs

FEMALE FROGS CAN OFTEN BE IDENTIFIED BECAUSE THEY ARE LARGER THAN MALES.

make their advertisement calls. When the females enter the breeding pond, the scramble begins. The larger males try to fight off the smaller males before the females arrive, forcing them into poor locations. In this way, the larger, more mature males tend to breed more often than the less dominant males.

Explosive breeding is a short-term activity, often lasting no longer than the time it takes the temporary breeding pools to dry up. Prolonged breeding, on the other hand, takes place during special seasons, or in some tropical regions, almost year-round. Prolonged breeding is again initiated by male advertising calls. However, males in this case do not aggressively mount females. Instead, they continue to sing until they are touched or nudged by a female to initiate amplexus.

How do females choose males? Evidence shows that in some species, females select males with deeper, louder voices and more complex songs. Frogs that sing in choruses often have a bout leader that starts and ends each round of the song. These bout leaders are known to be more successful in mating than their followers. Once the bout leader begins to mate, a new male takes over and is likely to get the next available female.

In some species of prolonged breeders, force rather than singing ability determines who will mate. Males jockey for position by butting, biting, and wrestling to gain control of breeding territory. But this doesn't mean that smaller or nondominant males are completely shut out of the process. In some frog species, such as the green tree frog, nondominant males steal mates from their more vocal rivals. They do this by waiting quietly while the calling male cries out. Then, when a female approaches, the quiet male rushes in to occupy the female before the calling male can take action.

Amplexus and Metamorphosis

It is important to recognize that amplexus is an *external* event. Typically, the male grasps the female from behind and waits for her to deposit the eggs. The male must release the sperm over the eggs at the exact moment they come out. If the eggs are allowed to hit the water, they instantly become coated with a protective jelly that prevents fertilization.

Once fertilized, the eggs begin to develop. Eggs are laid in

AMPLEXUS IN FLEISCHMANN'S GLASS FROG. A SINGLE DOMINANT MALE OF THIS SPECIES MAY MATE WITH SEVERAL FEMALES, LEAVING OTHER MALES WITHOUT A PARTNER.

groups called clutches. Clutches can be large clumps, long strings, or separate patches of eggs. Some species lay eggs directly onto the water surface. Others, such as the white-lipped frogs of Mexico, deposit eggs in a nest that the female makes by whipping up a secreted protein with water, in much the same way that you can whip up egg whites to make meringue.

Eggs develop in a variety of ways. A typical waterborne frog egg consists of an ovum (the living part of the egg) surrounded by layers of protective jelly. The ovum itself has two halves: the animal pole, which contains the growing tadpole cells, and the

Metamorphosis Day Book

HERE ARE THE BASIC STAGES OF METAMORPHOSIS FOLLOWED BY THOSE
FROGS THAT LAY EGGS IN WATER. AS WITH OTHER ASPECTS OF THE FROG
LIFE CYCLE, THESE STAGES DIFFER AMONG SPECIES.

Day 1: The eggs are laid. Within 30 to 60 minutes, the fertilized egg begins to divide. It goes from a single cell to 2, 4, 8, 16 cells and so on.

Days 2-6: Before long, the embryo in the animal pole grows over the vegetal pole and takes on a kidney shape. By now, it is rapidly consuming the food stored in the vegetal pole.

Day 7: When external gills and a mouth form, the tadpole is ready to hatch. The tadpole then secretes special enzymes that dissolve the protective jelly layers of the egg, allowing it to break free into the water. The tadpole may then lie low for several days, feeding on vegetable matter, waiting for its gills and muscular system to mature.

Day 15: The tadpole typically becomes a free-swimming organism around this time. Toothlike rasps inside the tadpole's mouth allow it to scrape algae and bacteria from the undersides of plant leaves.

Day 30: A flap grows over the tadpole's gills. This is the first step in a process in which the gills will become completely internalized. Tadpoles at this stage can live as social animals, often swimming together in schools like fish.

Day 45: Rear legs usually appear first, then front legs. The mouth begins to take on a froglike shape. The tail begins to shrink. The gills continue to recede into the body. The tadpole may now feed on dead insects as well as plants. Its long digestive system has begun to shorten as it readies itself for a carnivorous life on land.

Day 54: As the tail continues to shrink, the tadpole's legs continue to grow. When the lungs are fully functional, the tadpole leaves the water and becomes a froglet, or young frog.

vegetal pole, which contains yolk to feed the growing tadpole. Growth begins within an hour of fertilization. The transformation from egg to tadpole to adult frog is a continuous process that typically lasts for several weeks.

What Controls Metamorphosis?

During metamorphosis, an enormous number of changes take place. Gills disappear. Lungs grow. Body shape changes and limbs appear. Over time, a herbivorous aquatic animal—a tadpole   turns into a terrestrial, carnivorous animal—an adult frog. In essence, the tadpole "reinvents" itself from the inside out to become a new organism. What controls and orchestrates all of these remarkable changes?

Experiments indicate that thyroid hormone controls much of the process of metamorphosis. Thyroid hormone is a substance secreted by the tiny thyroid gland in the neck that influences the development and metabolism of all vertebrates, including human beings.

In 1912, scientist J. F. Gundernatsch conducted an experiment, feeding thyroid hormone from a horse to immature tadpoles. Amazingly, the tadpoles began to go through metamorphosis early. Later experiments showed that tadpoles whose thyroid glands were removed did not go through metamorphosis. These tadpoles without thyroid glands grew to a large size but did not mature or turn into adult frogs. On the other hand, the tadpoles that received extra thyroid hormone and went through metamorphosis early grew to be fully mature but very small frogs.

If thyroid hormone controls metamorphosis, what controls production of the hormone itself? It appears that both temperature and the chemical iodine can influence thyroid production. Iodine, long known to be an important part of the human diet because it controls thyroid hormone production, is also a critical part of the developing amphibian's diet. Amphibians that do not get an adequate amount of iodine in their diet fail to undergo metamorphosis successfully.

In many frog species, temperature controls the rate of metamorphosis. Most frogs complete metamorphosis in several weeks' time. But species that live in cold climates, such as North American bullfrogs, may take more than a full year to mature.

During cold spells, thyroid hormone level in tadpoles drops, delaying metamorphosis. This allows tadpoles that hatch during cold conditions to stay in the water as long as possible, postponing their move to the land. These cold-water tadpoles often grow to very large sizes before turning into frogs.

As temperatures warm, tadpoles produce more thyroid hormone, causing the rate of metamorphosis and development to increase. During unusually warm springs, thyroid hormone production in tadpoles reaches a maximum, allowing frogs to develop and begin life on land as quickly as possible. These warm-water tadpoles often reach maturity at very small sizes, growing larger only after they make their move to land.

Reproduction Modes

In all, herpetologists William Duellman and Linda Trueb have listed twenty-nine different reproduction modes for frogs. Here are descriptions of many of them.

Eggs Laid Directly in Water. Roughly half of all frogs, thirteen of the twenty-one families, lay their eggs in permanent bodies of standing water, such as lakes and ponds. This is thought to be the oldest and most primitve mode of reproduction. Egg clutches are laid singly, in strings, or large clumps. The advantage of laying eggs in clumps is to retain heat. Clumps are especially common in colder climates, such as the northern part of the United States.

Frogs also commonly lay their eggs in temporary pools, in streams and rivers, and in "hollows"—pools that collect in trees or hollowed out plants.

The South American Leptodactyl frogs and Australian Myobatrachids typically lay their eggs in foam nests in streams and pools. These nests protect the eggs from drying out, being

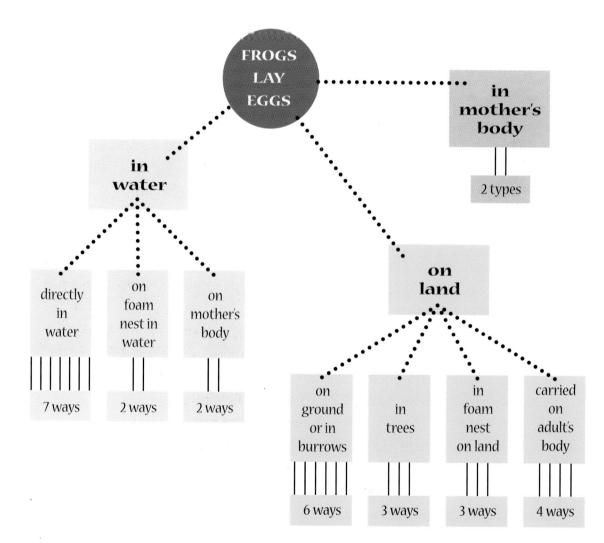

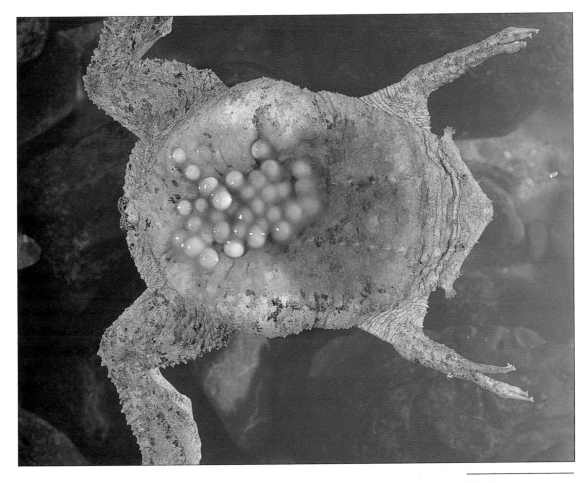

eaten by predators, or being damaged by ultraviolet radiation from the sun.

The most unusual mode of egg-laying in water is carried out by the Surinam toad, a member of the Pipid family. The Surinam toad female lays her eggs underwater in the sand. The male digs up the eggs and deposits them into "cubicles" on the female's back. The female then carries the embryos on her back for the next two to four months. When they hatch, the offspring crawl out of the mother's back as fully formed toadlets.

THE SURINAM TOAD IS ONE OF THE FEW FROG SPECIES THAT DOES NOT GO THROUGH A FREE-LIVING TADPOLE STAGE.

Eggs Laid Out of Water. Laying eggs on land represented a major step in becoming fully terrestrial. Frogs that lay their eggs on land typically lay fewer and larger eggs with more yolk than their water-laying relatives. The extra food reserve in larger eggs helps the young survive in the more hostile land environment.

Perhaps the simplest way to solve the problem of laying eggs on land is typified by many tree frogs that lay their eggs on branches above streams and ponds. When the embryos hatch, they drop into the water below and begin life as aquatic tadpoles.

Another way to lay eggs on land is to use a foam nest. Nests provide protection from all sorts of dangers that the land presents, often forming a thin crust on the outside while remaining moist on the inside. Some frogs lay terrestrial foam nests that are then washed away by seasonal floods, carrying tadpoles to water.

Several reproduction modes involve laying eggs that are subsequently taken to water in one way or another. Some Ranid frog lay their eggs on land, and the newly hatched tadpoles wriggle their way to the water. Some African frog species lay eggs in burrows, and then the female digs a tunnel for the tadpoles to nearby water. Poison dart frogs carry their eggs to nearby water after they hatch.

An even more bizarre reproductive system is carried out by Darwin's frog of Chile and Argentina. The female lays its eggs. When they begin to wriggle, the male sucks them up into his mouth and carries them around for several weeks. When the tadpoles mature, the male spits them out, fully developed. The

WHEN THE EGGS OF THIS CENTRAL AMERICAN LEAF FROG HATCH, THE TADPOLES WILL DROP INTO THE SAFETY OF THE WATER.

WITHIN EACH EGG, A TADPOLE DEVELOPS.

gastric brooding frog (which may now be extinct) also swallows its eggs. They develop inside the female's stomach, only to emerge six to seven weeks later as fully formed froglets.

Some species of eggs laid on land, including many Leptodactyls and some African Ranids, skip the tadpole stage completely. The eggs typically resemble reptile eggs, with tough outer membranes and a large supply of yolk. Direct development has the advantage of skipping the vulnerable tadpole stage. More important, it allows frogs to develop completely without the need of standing water.

In general, frogs do not spend a great deal of energy caring for their young. Some frogs lay thousands of eggs at a time. It is impractical to think that they could care for all, or any, of their offspring in any meaningful or realistic way.

Nevertheless, roughly 10 percent of all frog species *do* show some kind of parental care. You have seen some of the more impressive examples above in the behavior of the Surinam toad, Darwin's frog, and the midwife toad. In general, frogs that care for their offspring tend to have small broods. Instead of laying thousands of eggs that are left to fend for themselves, these frogs lay only a few eggs and try to make sure that each egg survives. Parental caregivers also tend to be small and to live in places that don't have standing water or other good breeding sites.

Examples of parental care include making nests, guarding eggs, keeping eggs wet, removing diseased eggs, moving eggs, carrying eggs on the body, and even, in the case of the strawberry poison dart frog, laying unfertilized eggs especially for the tadpoles to eat.

6 A Frog Gallery

> I'M NOBODY! WHO ARE YOU?
> ARE YOU—NOBODY, TOO? . . .
> HOW DREARY—TO BE—SOMEBODY!
> HOW PUBLIC—LIKE A FROG—
> TO TELL ONE'S NAME—THE LIVELONG JUNE—
> TO AN ADMIRING BOG!
>
> Poet Emily Dickinson

Previous chapters have looked at general characteristics shared by all frogs. While this focus is extremely valuable, it can only take you so far. To get to know frogs really well, you need to observe them up close. This chapter will introduce you to a gallery of selected frogs that live in the western hemisphere, from North to Central and South America. In the Americas and throughout the world there are, of course, many, many more.

Bullfrog

Did a monster bullfrog caught in 1949 actually tip the scales at an astonishing 7 pounds and 4 ounces (3.3 kg)? *The Guinness Book of Animal Facts and Feats* claims that such a bullfrog existed. Otherwise, the official heavyweight record for bullfrogs stands at a more modest 1 pound 4 ounces (0.56 kg)—still a *very* big frog.

In fact, the bullfrog is North America's largest native frog.

BULLFROGS HAVE BEEN FOUND WITH BABY ALLIGATORS IN THEIR STOMACHS.

(Cane toads are larger but they are not native to the continent.) Measuring up to 6 inches (15 cm) in length, bullfrogs are the reigning giants of their pond and lake habitats.

Bullfrogs are not timid. They are tough and aggressive, often resorting to wrestling and head-butting to defend their pond-front territories against intruders. However, bullfrogs do not get their name from being bullishly combative but rather from their distinctive bullhorn bass voice.

During the spring mating season, the males' foghornlike calls lure females to the breeding sites from up to a half-mile away. Female bullfrogs may lay up to 20,000 eggs at a time. Unlike most other frog species, bullfrog tadpoles in northern locations take up to two years to complete metamorphosis, wintering through their first year as tadpoles at the bottom of the pond. Once they become adults, bullfrogs have a life span of up to twenty-five years.

Bullfrogs are excellent swimmers and such powerful leapers that they often come away as the winners of frog-jumping contests. Bullfrogs are also skilled hunters, eating such varied prey as insects, turtles, crayfish, fish, small snakes, and even baby ducks. Herpetologist Mary Dickerson states that a bullfrog will eat "any object that he can swallow." Indeed, the introduction of bullfrogs to nonnative locations in the western United States has often had a harmful effect on populations of local amphibians and reptiles.

Spring Peeper

In the northeastern United States there is no more distinctive sign that spring has arrived than the jingling *pe-e-ep pe-e-ep* choruses of the spring peeper. These tiny 1.5-inch (4-cm) tree frogs hibernate during the cold winter months and announce their emergence in February or March in almost earsplitting choruses.

A full-blown spring peeper chorus is created by hundreds of unseen frogs, all of which come to a complete halt at the appearance of an intruder. However, if the intruder stays still the peepers will very soon resume their singing.

The songs themselves are generated by individual trios of male frogs. Typically, the first member of the trio sings an A-note. The second trio member responds with a G-sharp. Back and forth they go: A-G-sharp, A-G-sharp until the third member chimes in with a B-note producing the complete A-G-sharp-B sequence, which is then repeated over and over again. This same sequence is sung by dozens of different trios, creating a jangling, bell-like chorus.

HARD TO SEE, EASY TO HEAR: SPRING PEEPERS ARE OFTEN DIFFICULT TO FIND BECAUSE THEY STOP SINGING WHEN AN INTRUDER COMES NEAR.

Females eventually respond to the males' song, often swimming out to their partner and touching him on the back to initiate amplexus. Dominant males push other males to the sidelines, forcing them to wait their turn to mate. Some evidence points to female peepers' preferring a mate that generates fast-paced calling songs rather than loud or deep-voiced songs.

Peepers have vocal sacs that inflate to huge, balloonlike proportions when calling. The frogs can be identified by their tan, reddish-brown, or dull green color and by the distinctive X-shaped pattern across their back.

American Toad

The American toad presents an ideal image of "toadishness." It is short, squat, slow afoot, dull in color, and its skin is covered with bumps and warts. Is it ugly? That depends on the eye of the observer. Gardeners in the eastern United States, the American toad's home range, tend to hold the creature in highest regard—not for its handsome profile, but rather, for its ability to devour pests and insects.

The American toad is indeed a voracious eater of garden pests. One study estimated that 88 percent of the toad's diet consisted of insects that were harmful to garden plants, including mosquitoes, locusts, grasshoppers, snails, slugs, and hairy caterpillars. This is why the toad is a highly prized creature in France, where gardeners actually purchase toads and set them free in their gardens to control pests. One examination of the contents of a toad's stomach revealed a total of forty-eight insects, including ants, moths, weevils, sow bugs, beetles, grasshoppers, and crickets.

Much of the toad's disagreeable reputation may be based on its toxic defense system. Picking up a toad may trigger the

THE AMERICAN
TOAD MAY NOT BE
HARMFUL TO PEOPLE,
BUT THE TOAD'S
POISONS CAN BE
FATAL TO A DOG
THAT IS FOOLISH
ENOUGH TO TRY TO
EAT ONE.

secretion of a milky fluid from the parotoid gland between the creature's eyes. Animals such as dogs may find this poison particularly troublesome, as it has been known to cause respiratory paralysis in smaller victims. Humans do not suffer any life-threatening effects from toad poison, but it is always a good idea to wash one's hands after handling a toad.

In fact, the toad's skin has been described as a "drugstore" full of chemically active substances. These substances include anesthetics that kill pain, stimulants that increase heart rate, various poisons, and even some chemicals that are reported to induce intoxicating effects on some misguided (if not downright stupid) users who indulge in "toad-licking" and "toad-smoking." Needless to say, these practices are not only disgusting, they are also unwise and unhealthy.

Breeding in the American toad is quite an explosive affair, with great masses of wriggling toads piled on top of one another in a formation called a knot. The rapidity with which toads get together in breeding ponds after a big rainstorm is so startling that it has become the source of tales of toads "raining" down from the sky. The male toad's advertising call is sometimes described as "sweet" and "musical," even though when in full swing the chorus creates a considerable racket.

In captivity, the American toad makes a fine pet. One particularly long-lived specimen was reported to have still been going strong at the age of thirty-six, when it met its end in an untimely accident.

Poison Dart Frogs

By far the most colorful and dangerous of all of the world's 3,500 different frog species are 135 varieties of poison dart frogs of genus *Dendrobates* and *Phyllobates*. These small, dazzling creatures live a very "unfroglike" existence.

While most frogs lead a fairly hidden and secretive existence, poison dart frogs live conspicuously in their Central and South American rainforest habitats, unconcerned, for the most part, by the threat of predators. While most frogs are active at night, poison dart frogs are active during the day, when their multicolored skin is most highly visible. While most frogs secrete a modest amount of poison from their skin, poison dart frogs secrete poison so potent that as little as 0.00001 grams can be enough to kill a human being.

In fact, the blazing coloration of the poison dart frog is no accident. Instead, it serves as a warning to forest-dwellers to steer clear of these brightly colored species. The toxins themselves are nerve poisons that open the membranes of nerve and muscle cells, leaving the nerves unable to transmit impulses and the muscles in a state of permanent contraction. Most victims of poison dart frogs therefore perish from heart or respiratory failure.

Until recently, the greatest enemy to poison dart frogs were the South American Indians, who used their poison in blowguns for hunting birds, monkeys, and other game. The hunters obtained the frogs by imitating their calls using whistles, thereby luring them into capture. In the past few years, the hunters have become less dependent on blowguns for hunting. This has resulted in a decrease in the number of poison dart frogs killed each year by hunters.

STRAWBERRY POISON DART FROGS ARE TYPICALLY RED, BUT THESE FROGS ALSO COME IN OTHER COLORS, INCLUDING GREEN, YELLOW, ORANGE, OR BLACK AND WHITE.

As breeders, poison dart frogs display a number of remarkable behaviors. In some species, newly hatched tadpoles crawl up the legs of an adult male, who then carries them to the water-filled center of a bromeliad plant where they undergo metamorphosis. *Dendrobates histrionocus* is an example of a frog that actually feeds its young—a rare occurrence in the amphibian world. As the tadpoles develop in bromeliad cups, females of the *D. histrionocus* species bring sterile, unfertilized eggs for them to feed on.

Cane Toad

In 1930, the sugarcane fields of Puerto Rico were overrun with beetles and other pests. Nothing the plantation owners did could control the pests, and they ended up destroying millions of dollars worth of valuable crops.

Enter the cane toad, *Bufo marinus*. It was introduced to Puerto Rico in 1932. "Here was an animal," says Australian herpetologist Michael J. Tyler, "that bred like rabbits, required no maintenance, and, without question, devoured every insect it encountered." Before long the cane toad experiment was judged a success. Puerto Rico's pest population was under control, thanks to the cane toad.

Soon, cane toads were introduced to other sugarcane growing regions of the world, including Hawaii, the Philippines, and other Pacific islands. By 1935, Australia brought cane toads to its own cane fields. This time, the results weren't as positive. The huge (up to 10 inches, or 25 cm) toads had soon overrun the countryside, appearing everywhere like a writhing horde. The problem in Australia was that the toads had no natural predator, nothing to keep their population in check. They ate pests, but their voracious appetites also encompassed other nonpest

organisms, including fish, birds, and other amphibians.

Before 1930, the cane toad's habitat was limited to Trinidad and French Guiana. Now it is seen over much of the southern hemisphere. The lesson of the cane toad is a mixed one. While the experiment was not a total failure, it did point out the dangers and concerns of introducing species into habitats in which they don't naturally live.

Ornate Horned Frog

Most frogs are rather shy and retiring creatures, lacking the temperament or means to face the world aggressively. Not so the ornate horned frog. This massive (up to 7 inches [18 cm] in length) bruiser looks tough, acts tough, and when all is said and done, turns out to be a pretty tough and ferocious character, especially for a frog.

With its hostile scowl, horned eyelids, gaping mouth, and blocky, Sumo wrestler body, the ornate horned frog projects the image of the fierce and fearless fighter that it is. Unlike other frog

species, the ornate horned frog doesn't hesitate to attack intruders, jumping at them so it can clamp on its viselike jaws. Once attached, its powerful jaws and sharp teeth can inflict considerable damage even on larger victims. It can be as difficult to dislodge as a snapping turtle or a bulldog.

Native to Argentina, southern Brazil, and Uruguay, the ornate horned frog has recently become very popular in pet shops. However, keeping more than one specimen in the same cage may be a fatal mistake, as the ravenous appetites of ornate horned frogs will drive them to eat almost *anything* when hungry, including other ornate horned frogs.

Spadefoot Toad

Spadefoot toads live in deserts and arid areas in North America (and in Asia, Europe, and northwestern Africa). At 3 inches (7.5 cm) long or less, they are tiny. But the tough, horny spades on their hind legs allow spadefoots to dig backward through loose soil with remarkable speed and efficiency. When threatened, spadefoots can bury themselves in a matter of seconds.

Spadefoots seem to remain beneath the surface for weeks. However, most of them come up at night for food and water. During true droughts, spadefoots seal themselves off in underground chambers waterproofed with body secretions. At the first sign of moisture they come to the surface.

Spadefoots are especially explosive breeders. During the breeding season, reproductive behavior starts immediately after a hard rain. The males stand in temporary rain pools making their *wa-a-ank wa-a-ank* calls. Mating is often a frenzied affair, with females swimming out to meet males in their puddles.

Because they live in such dry climates, reproduction for spadefoots is often a rushed affair. Spadefoot tadpoles hatch rapidly. Their food supply is often so limited that some spadefoot tadpoles resort to cannibalism. The tadpoles develop quickly and leave the water well before their tails begin to shrink. All of these measures are taken for one end: to reach the adult, terrestrial stage of the life cycle before the water dries up.

COUCH'S SPADEFOOT TOAD LIVES IN THE ARIZONA DESERT.

7 Frogs in Trouble

> YOU DON'T LIVE IN A WORLD ALL ALONE.
>
> Nobel Peace Prize Winner Albert Schweitzer

Twice a year the golden toads would gather to breed high in the mountains near a little town in Costa Rica called Monteverde. Witnesses to the event have described it as "astonishing," "thrilling," and "magnificent." Hundreds of toads would swarm the forest floor, each one so brilliant, so gorgeous, that it gleamed like a tiny jewel.

People came from far and wide to view them. Twice a year they made the trek to an isolated ridge called El Brillante, and the golden toads never failed to show up.

MISSING: THE GOLDEN TOAD OF COSTA RICA

Then one year the people came and there were no golden toads. Where had they gone? Was something wrong? And more important, was the same thing happening to other frog species around the world?

The golden toads of Costa Rica began to disappear in 1987. Before that year, they had always been plentiful during each breeding season. Then something happened. At first, herpetologists blamed the absence of the toads on some unusual occurrence, such as a drought or storm. But as the years passed, the golden toads did not return.

In 1990, herpetologists from around the world gathered in Irvine, California. The stated purpose of their meeting was to discuss the results of their latest research projects. But as the meeting progressed, many of the scientists had disturbing stories to tell. Like the golden toads of Costa Rica, frogs from other parts of the world were also vanishing.

What was going on? The scientists would have liked to have sounded an alarm right then, but they needed more data. After all, extreme fluctuations in frog populations were not unheard of. Perhaps the declines were just part of a natural up-and-down cycle that would soon turn around.

A Global Problem

Since 1990, one clear fact has emerged. For many amphibian species, the decline is very real. It is not a temporary phase or simply the "down" part of a natural population cycle. Dozens of different frog species have been affected, including California red-leggeds, Cascade frogs of the Pacific northwest, harlequin frogs of Central America, leopard frogs of Canada, arroyo toads of the desert Southwest, Colorado river toads, mountain yellow-legged frogs, western spadefoot toads, and many others.

CASCADES FROG, *RANA CASCADAE*

HARLEQUIN FROG OF CENTRAL AMERICA, *ATELOPUS VARIUS*

FROGS SUCH AS THIS NORTHERN LEOPARD FROG IN MINNESOTA HAVE BEEN FOUND
WITH DEFORMED LIMBS OR THE WRONG NUMBER OF LIMBS. SO FAR, SCIENTISTS HAVE
NOT FOUND A CAUSE FOR THESE ABNORMALITIES.

At first, scientists looked for a single cause common to each
decline. Habitat destruction seemed a likely culprit. Each day,
acres of rain forest were being lost. Wetlands were being
drained. Forests were being bulldozed to make way for development. Pollution in all its different forms—pesticides, fertilizers,
toxic waste, acid rain, and so on—was also destroying amphibian habitats.

But while habitat destruction was a serious problem, it was clearly not the whole story. To understand why, take the case of the golden toads. The golden toads lived in a remote mountain area. Their habitat, for the most part, was untouched and unspoiled. Yet the golden toads, and many other frog species living in remote areas, were disappearing as fast, and in some cases, even faster than species in densely populated regions. What was killing them off?

A Breakthrough—of Sorts

Most scientists didn't pay much attention to Dr. Andrew Blaustein's hypothesis regarding ultraviolet radiation when he first proposed it in 1991. Blaustein's idea was that frog communities were being devastated by ultraviolet (UV) light.

Blaustein's reasoning was as follows. Ultraviolet radiation comes from the sun. Most UV rays are fairly harmless. But one type, the UV-B rays, is deadly to biological tissue.

Normally, a layer of ozone high in the atmosphere protects Earth from UV-B rays. But ozone reacts with chemicals called CFCs (chlorofluorocarbons) that were widely used as refrigerants from the 1930s to the 1980s. The CFCs escaped into the air and reacted with the ozone high in the atmosphere, creating gaps and weaknesses in the ozone layer through which deadly UV-B rays could pass to Earth below.

Blaustein's hypothesis was that frogs would be especially vulnerable to UV-B rays because both their skin and their eggs are unprotected. When Blaustein exposed a mountain frog species to UV-B light, he found that many of them did not survive. At last, the mystery was beginning to unravel. The frogs were being killed by ultraviolet light. Or were they?

A Messy Problem

In science, some problems are easy to solve. Others are messy and complicated. Such was the case with trying to discover the cause of declining frog populations. While Blaustein's UV-B experiments were initially encouraging, they didn't tell the whole story. Yes, UV-B light did appear to harm some mountain frogs that basked in the sun to get warm. But golden toads, for example, were not sun-baskers. Their exposure to the sun's rays was extremely limited. So it was very unlikely that UV-B rays were the cause of the golden toads' demise.

Scientists began to look for other causes of frog decline. There was no shortage of suspects. Habitat destruction may not have killed the golden toads of Costa Rica, but such things as river damming, residential housing development, rain forest destruction, swamp drainage, logging, mining, and highway construction could still have been major factors in the decline of other frog populations.

And those frogs whose habitats weren't being destroyed directly may have been harmed by pollution—including ground-water contamination, heavy metal residues, and sewage—as well as disease germs, fungus, parasites, viruses, and bacteria.

Finally, such things as global warming, the El Niño ocean current, and other natural climatic events may have created droughts, floods, and extreme temperatures that were damaging frog communities.

In summary, some, all, or any of these factors may have played a role in the disappearance of the frogs. But it is unlikely that any single factor has been the sole cause behind all the declines, most of which continue to this day.

In fact, evidence now points to the possibility that different frog species are affected by different factors. One type of frog may be harmed by UV-B light. Another frog, in a different area, may be affected by acid rain. Still another species might be declining because of habitat destruction.

As if this weren't complicated enough, in many cases a combination of effects may be influencing events. Thus, recent evidence shows that frogs in places as far apart as Australia and Central America were both being killed off by a fungus. Was this fungus acting on its own, or were such factors as heat and drought, UV-B radiation, or pollution weakening the frogs so they were not able to fight off the disease that the fungus brought on? Only time and more research will give the answer to this and many other important questions.

Why Frogs?

Whatever its causes—the great decline in amphibian populations poses many serious and puzzling questions. For example, why should amphibians be harmed more than other creatures? After all, these organisms all live together in the same ecosystem. If the ecosystem is damaged, it stands to reason that *all* animal communities should be affected, not just some.

The answer to this question remains hazy. It appears that amphibians *are* being killed off more readily than other animal groups. The question then becomes, *why?* Why should amphibians be more vulnerable to environmental damage than birds, mammals, or other groups?

When you consider that amphibians lead a dual life—neither fully terrestrial nor fully aquatic—you begin to understand why they might be singled out for destruction more than other groups. Since amphibians live and breed both on land and in water, they are twice as vulnerable as animals that live only in water or on land.

This has led some scientists to suggest that amphibians function as a bioindicator, an organism whose general well-being signals the state of an entire ecosystem. Thus, if a bioindicator species is healthy, you would expect its ecosystem to be healthy. On the other hand, if the bioindicator population is drastically decreasing, you would conclude that the ecosystem must have some serious problems.

Bioindicators are like the canaries that miners used in nineteenth-century coal mines. Canaries do not breathe well in oxygen-poor environments. Consequently, when the canary began to swoon, miners knew that it was time to leave the mine, even before they sensed that their own safety was threatened.

Is it time to "leave the mine"? Perhaps not, but many biologists believe that frogs and amphibians do function as twenty-first-century mine canaries—not only for single, isolated ecosystems but for the entire Earth as a grand, composite ecosystem.

Does It Matter?

In the end, the decline of frogs and amphibians boils down to a single question: does it matter that frogs are disappearing? The answer to this question depends on your point of view. To those who see amphibians as the ultimate mine canaries for the entire planet, the message is clear. If frogs are disappearing, then the whole system must be in grave trouble, perhaps even beyond repair.

But many biologists are cautious. While they admit that the disappearance of frogs is a disturbing trend, they also point out that the situation is nothing new. Frog species have gone extinct in the past. They will no doubt continue to go extinct in the future.

What does it mean when a forest that was once alive with the croaking of hundreds of frogs suddenly goes silent? Is it something we can ignore? Or do we ignore it only at our peril?

Most thoughtful biologists ultimately see the great frog decline as a warning. The world can withstand the loss of a few frog species. What it cannot withstand are the conditions under which species will continue to be lost.

Perhaps the best way to approach the situation is to see it from the frog's point of view. Earth has been a frog-friendly place for millions of years. Will it continue to be a place where frogs can survive and flourish for millions of years in the future? Only time will tell.

A WINDOW ON THE WORLD. WHAT DOES THE HEALTH OF THE WORLD'S FROG POPULATIONS TELL US ABOUT THE HEALTH OF OUR ENVIRONMENT?

Glossary

adaptation—an acquired trait that helps an organism survive in its environment

amniotic—eggs that contain an inner layer of watery amniotic fluid and a hard outer shell that help the embryo survive outside of water

amphibian—an animal with a smooth, porous outer skin that spends part of its life on land and part of its life in the water

amplexus—external fertilization in frogs; the act of depositing sperm on eggs as they are released

Anura—amphibian group that includes all frogs; from the Greek for "tailless ones"

camouflage—use of color, pattern, and shape to blend in with one's surroundings to escape the notice of predators

carbon dioxide—the gas that is released by organisms during the process of respiration

cloaca—single opening into which urinary, digestive, and reproductive systems empty in amphibians

clutch—a group of eggs

dehydration—the process of removing water from something

diffusion—passive movement of a substance from where it is plentiful to where it is scarce

ectotherm—cold-blooded; an animal that cannot regulate its body temperature using its own internal heat

endotherm—warm-blooded; an animal that regulates its body temperature using its own internal heat

estivation—heat hibernation; prolonged escape from heat by burrowing or other means

exoskeleton—rigid outer skeleton that covers the bodies of mollusks, insects, and other arthropods

explosive breeders—frogs that breed for a short period of time at a predictable season of the year

fertilization—the combining of sperm and egg to make a new organism

flash colors—very bright colors that are designed to startle predators

fossil—the preserved remains of an organism that once lived

habitat—the place in which an organism makes its home

herpetologist—a scientist who studies amphibians and reptiles

hydration—the act of adding water to an organism or nonliving thing

impermeable—not allowing water and other substances to pass through

kingdom—one of the six main divisions of living things: bacteria, a bacteria-like group, single-celled organisms, fungi, plants, and animals

larva—an immature form of an organism (plural: larvae)

metamorphosis—the developmental process in which a frog (or other organism) changes its body form from larva to adult

mucus—a sticky, protective liquid

niche—the place an organism occupies in its ecosystem with respect to the food chain, resource use, and actual physical space

nictitating membrane—a thin covering that slides down over the eyes

ovum—an egg (plural: ova)

oxidize—to burn by combining with oxygen

oxygen—an important gas that is a key ingredient in air and is needed by almost all living things to burn fuel in order to get energy during respiration

ozone—a gas that exists in a thin layer high in the atmosphere that protects living things from harmful ultraviolet radiation

permeable—water and other substances are able to penetrate

phylum—a major subdivision of living things; examples: amphibians, reptiles

pigment—a colored substance that exists in the skin or outer layer of an organism

predator—an organism that eats other organisms (prey)

prey—an organism that is eaten by another organism (predator)

prolonged breeders—frogs that breed over a long period of time

respiration—the process of taking in food and oxygen and burning them to obtain energy

species—a particular kind of organism that breeds with others of the same kind

tadpole—the immature form of a frog; a frog larva

tetrapod—a four-legged animal

thyroid hormone—a hormone that affects metabolism and development of frogs and other organisms

ultraviolet radiation—radiation from the high-energy part of the spectrum that comes from the sun and that can be harmful to living things

vertebrate—animals that have backbones; a subphylum of the chordate phylum

Species Checklist

Frogs have both common and scientific names. Common names can be confusing. More than one common name may be used for the same frog, and some common names refer to whole groups of frogs. This list, which is in alphabetical order by common name, will help you find additional information about many of the frogs mentioned in this book.

Common names are usually written in lower case, unless it is taken from a proper name. Scientific names, which are in Latin, should be italicized, with the first, or generic, name capitalized and the second, which identifies the species, in lowercase.

African clawed frog *Xenopus laevis*

American toad *Bufo americanus*

barking tree frog *Hyla gratoisa*

Brazilian tree frog; slender-legged tree frog
 Osteocephalus subtilis

Budgett's frog *Lepidobatrachus laevis*

bullfrog *Rana catesbeiana*

California red-legged frog *Aurora draytonii*

cane toad *Bufo marinus*

carpenter frog *Rana virgatipes*

Cascade frog *Rana cascadae*

Colorado River toad *Bufo alvarius*

common toad *Bufo americanus*

Couch's spadefoot toad *Scaphiopus couchi*

Cranwell's horned frog *Ceratophrys cranwelli*

Darwin's frog *Rhinoderma darwini*

Eastern spadefoot toad *Scaphiopus holbrookii holbrookii*

edible frog *Rana esculenta*

European common frog *Rana temporaria*

European common toad *Bufo bufo*

European tree frog *Hyla arborea*

Fort Randolph robber frog *Eleutherodactylus gaigea*

glass frog *Centrolenella fleischmanni*

gold frog *Psyllophryne didactyla*

golden poison dart frog *Phyllobates terribilis*

golden toad *Bufo periglens*

goliath frog *Canraua goliath*

gray tree frog *Hyla chrysoscelis*

green frog *Rana clamitans melanota*

green tree frog *Hyla cinerea*

harlequin frog *Atelopus flavescens*

Hochstetter's New Zealand frog *Leiopelma hochstetteri*

horned toad *Bufo ceratophrys*

lovely poison dart frog *Phyllobates lugubris*

masked tree frog *Smilisca phaeota*

midwife toad *Alytes obstetricanus*

mountain yellow-legged frog *Rana muscosa*

northern leopard frog *Rana pipiens*

oriental fire-bellied toad *Bombina orientalis*

ornate horned frog *Ceratophrys ornata*

panther toad *Bufo regularis*

pickerel frog *Rana palustris*

pig frog *Rana grylio*

plains spadefoot toad *Spea bombifrons*

red-eyed tree frog *Agalychnis callidryas*

southern cricket frog *Acris gryllus gryllus*

southern gastric brooding frog *Rheobatrachus silus*

southern leopard frog *Rana utricularia*

southwestern arroyo toad *Bufo microscaphus californicus*

spring peeper *Pseudacris crucifer*

strawberry poison dart frog *Dendrobates pumilio*

Surinam toad *Pipa pipa*

wood frog *Rana sylvatica*

Further Research

A tremendous amount has been written about frogs. Here you will find a list of books and web sites to get you started.

Books for Young People

Clarke, Barry. *Amphibian*. New York: Knopf, 1993.

Gerholdt, James E. *Frogs*. Minneapolis, MN: ABDO, 1994.

Himmelman, John. *A Wood Frog's Life*. Danbury, CT: Children's Press, 1998.

Hunt, Joni P. *A Chorus of Frogs*. Parsippany, NJ: Silver Burdett, 1994.

Johnson, Sylvia A. *Tree Frogs*. Minneapolis, MN: Lerner, 1986.

Parker, Steve. *Frogs & Toads*. San Francisco: Sierra Club Children's, 1994.

Pascoe, Elaine. *Tadpoles*. Woodbridge, CT: Blackbirch, 1996.

Web Sites

Amphibian Information Website
http://monitoring2.pwrc.nbs.gov/amphibs

Froglog
http://acs-info.open.ac.uk/info/newsletters/FROGLOG.html
(newsletter of the Declining Amphibian Populations Task Force of the World Conservation Union's Species Survival Commision)

The Frog Store
http://frog.simplenet.com/froggy

Frog, Toad & Treefrog Links Index
http://dencity.com/bombina/froglinks

Frog Web
http://www.frogweb.gov/index.html

Frogland
http://allaboutfrogs.org

NARCAM: North American Reporting Center for Amphibian Malformations
http://www.npwrc.usgs.gov/narcam

The Somewhat Amusing World of Frogs
http://www.csu.edu.au/faculty/commerce/account/frogs/frog.htm

Westward Frog!
http://ice.ucdavis.edu/Toads/texthtml/wwfrog.html
(information about threats to amphibian survival and the decline of amphibian populations, particularly in California)

Bibliography

These books were used by the author while researching this book. Many of them are suitable for a young reader, especially if used sparingly for reference.

Badger, David P. *Frogs*. Stillwater, MN: Voyageur Press, 1995.
    A lively account with gorgeous photographs

Dickerson, Mary C. *The Frog Book*. New York: Dover, 1906, 1969.
    A true classic; first published in 1906

Duellman, William and Linda Trueb. *Biology of Amphibians*. Baltimore: Johns Hopkins University Press, 1994.
    The authority on frogs; very scientific and difficult but includes everything about frogs

Mattison, Chris. *Frogs & Toads of the World*. New York: Facts on File, 1987.
    A highly informative source

Phillips, Kathryn. *Tracking the Vanishing Frogs*. New York: St. Martin's Press, 1994.
    Tells the story of the golden toads and other vanishing frogs

Simon, Hilda. *Frogs and Toads of the World*. Philadelphia: Lippincott, 1975.
    A good introduction to frogs

Index

Page numbers for illustrations are in **boldface**.

About the Author

DAN GREENBERG raised tadpoles as a twelve year old and was delighted when his young amphibians turned into froglets. Greenberg has written numerous books for people of all ages, in science and in other fields. His well-received series 30 Wild and Wonderful Math Stories now has six titles.

Mr. Greenberg's idea of good fun is to take a walk along the edge of a pond and sneak up on bullfrogs as they bask in the sun. He lives in New Rochelle, New York, with his wife and two children.